JULIA I

MONEY LOVES
You

TRANSFORM YOUR RELATIONSHIP WITH MONEY AND GROW YOUR WEALTH

MONEY LOVES You

TRANSFORM YOUR RELATIONSHIP WITH MONEY AND GROW YOUR WEALTH
Copyright © 2023 by Julia M. Carlson

All rights reserved. No part of this publication may be reproduced, stored in a retrieval system, or transmitted in any form or by any means, electronic, mechanical, photocopying, recording, or otherwise, without written permission of the publisher or author, except for the use of brief quotations in a book review.

Although the author and publisher have made every effort to ensure that the information in this book was correct at press time, the author and publisher do not assume and hereby disclaim any liability to any party for any loss, damage, or disruption caused by errors or omissions, whether such errors or omissions result from negligence, accident, or any other cause.

Adherence to all applicable laws and regulations, including international, federal, state and local governing professional licensing, business practices, advertising, and all other aspects of doing business in the US, Canada or any other jurisdiction is the sole responsibility of the reader and consumer.

Neither the author nor the publisher assumes any responsibility or liability whatsoever on behalf of the consumer or reader of this material. Any perceived slight of any individual or organization is purely unintentional.

The resources in this book are provided for informational purposes only and should not be used to replace the specialized training and professional judgment of a health care or mental health care professional.

Neither the author nor the publisher can be held responsible for the use of the information provided within this book. Please always consult a trained professional before making any decision regarding treatment of yourself or others.

To request permissions, contact the publisher at publish@joapublishing.com or julia@juliamcarlson.com

Hardcover ISBN: 978-1-961098-40-4
Paperback ISBN: 978-1-961098-38-1
eBook ISBN: 978-1-961098-39-8
Printed in the USA.

Joan of Arc Publishing
Meridian, ID 83646
www.joapublishing.com

ABOUT THE AUTHOR

Before we dive in, let me share a little about me. I am an entrepreneur at heart. I launched into the financial services field at the age of 19 and at age 23 started my own business in a male-dominated finance industry. As a devoted wife to my husband, Chris, for over 27 years, a mother to three amazing children, and a business owner, I see now how bold that decision was, but at the time it felt like it was the only choice I could make in order to realize my dreams. I now have over 27 years of experience helping individuals, families, and business owners with their wealth-management and financial-planning needs.

What exactly does that mean? My team and I help people strengthen their financial futures by creating personalized investment portfolios and tailored strategies that aim to grow their wealth over time. The goal of this planning is to ensure they can become financially independent, using their money in ways that maximize their personal values throughout their lives and for generations to come.

For business owners, we specialize in proactive tax strategies and exit planning designed to increase profitability, create a lasting legacy, and instill confidence. This business planning allows the owners to build wealth inside and outside their businesses.

My firms, Financial Freedom Wealth Management Group and Freedom Tax, serve over 1700 clients across the United States. I have been honored to be recognized for excellence throughout my career, including being ranked by Forbes as one of America's Top Women Wealth Advisors.[1]

I am passionate about living life fully in the present—creating memories now instead of waiting until someday—and actively living the concepts discussed in this book. I have been invited to speak at many different events on a variety of topics including: how I built an eight-figure[2] business while integrating life as a mom; how to lead an extraordinary team; and inspiring business owners to create scale in their business by firing themselves, resulting in increased personal freedom and business success.

While these stages were large and I was speaking to many, my passion remains helping people transform their personal finances. Nothing shocks me: the millionaire that didn't diversify their investments and lost it all, the young couple filled with despair because they have massive amounts of debt, the business owner receiving 30 million dollars when they sold their business they built from nothing, the couple who inherited millions and spent it all within a few years, and the empty nester with little retirement savings and a lot of ground to cover to catch up their savings.

I've experienced all levels and types of money situations and stories; I've seen it all. And if I could give one piece of helpful advice to inspire others from my beautiful 27-year career it would be this: Money Loves You.

Let's dive in.

Disclosures:

[1] The Forbes ranking of America's Top Women Wealth Advisors, developed by SHOOK research, is based on a ranking algorithm that includes completion of an online survey, telephone and in-person due diligence interviews, client retention, industry experience, review of compliance records and U4s, firm nominations; and quantitative criteria, including: assets under management and revenue generated for their firm. This ranking was applied for by the advisor, and not LPL Financial. Assets under management information includes advisory and brokerage assets serviced by Ms. Carlson through LPL Financial. Investment performance is not a criteria due to varying client objectives and risk tolerances, and lack of advisors audited performance records. The rating may not be representative of any one client's experience and is not indicative of the financial advisor's future performance. Neither Forbes nor SHOOK Research receives a fee in exchange for rankings. The full list of Forbes Top Women Wealth Advisors is available at www.forbes.com/lists/top-women-advisors.

[2] Third-party business valuation as of May 17, 2022.

The opinions voiced in this material are for general information only and are not intended to provide specific advice or recommendations for any individual. All performance referenced is historical and is no guarantee of future results. All indices are unmanaged and may not be invested into directly.

There is no guarantee that a diversified portfolio will enhance overall returns or outperform a non-diversified portfolio. Diversification does not protect against market risk.

Stock investing includes risks, including fluctuating prices and loss of principal.

Julia is an Investment Advisor Representative and Registered Principal with LPL Financial. Securities and Advisory Services offered through LPL Financial, a Registered Investment Advisor. Member FINRA/SIPC.

TABLE OF CONTENTS

INTRODUCTION 13

CHAPTER ONE
CAN MONEY LOVE? 17

CHAPTER TWO
IT IS ALL POSSIBLE 23

CHAPTER THREE
PREPARE FOR GROWTH 31

CHAPTER FOUR
UNDERSTANDING THE CONSCIOUS, SUBCONSCIOUS,
AND SUPERCONSCIOUS MIND 41

CHAPTER FIVE
READY TO RECEIVE 49

CHAPTER SIX
TRUST YOURSELF 55

CHAPTER SEVEN
TRANSFORM YOUR BELIEFS 63

CHAPTER EIGHT
REVEAL YOUR MONEY IDENTITY 85

CHAPTER NINE
CREATE YOUR FREEDOM NOW 97

CHAPTER TEN
SHATTER CONVENTIONAL RULES 105

CHAPTER ELEVEN
INSPIRED WEALTH™ 113

CHAPTER TWELVE
FREEDOM NUMBER™ 119

CHAPTER THIRTEEN
SEE TRUTH 131

CHAPTER FOURTEEN
WELCOME TO THE ANTI-BUDGET! 141

CHAPTER FIFTEEN
FINANCIAL SEASONS™ 151

CHAPTER SIXTEEN
RELATIONSHIPS AND MONEY 159

CHAPTER SEVENTEEN
HERE IS WHAT IS NOW POSSIBLE 171

CHAPTER EIGHTEEN
ALLOW MONEY TO LOVE YOU 177

A NOTE TO THE READER

Yes. Money does love you. Maybe you don't believe me. Maybe this title stirred a whole range of emotions within you: humor, anger, disbelief, or wonder. How can I possibly bring love into the subject of money? And I would ask, how can I not? There are people who will say money is the root of all evil and you might have lots of reasons why money can't love you. I understand.

This is a different type of money book. Money will help you do good. I am here to help you shatter conventional rules of money (I can't wait for you to experience the anti-budget method) and to be your guide as you establish a new empowering relationship with money, one that aims to create wealth and abundance for you and your family. Let's explore the future of what is possible for you.

INTRODUCTION

On that fateful day at the Wharton School at the University of Pennsylvania, I faced a daunting challenge: stepping out of my cozy hotel room and into an unknown place where I didn't feel I belonged . . . a university classroom. My heart raced as I quickly walked the Ivy League campus toward the Wharton Quad Buildings. I was filled with a mix of excitement, fear, and anxiety, with these nagging doubts echoing in my mind: I don't belong here. I'm not smart enough.

Months earlier, I had received a special invitation to attend an executive education program at The Wharton School. The anticipation was electrifying, but my imposter syndrome threatened to steal the spotlight. Twenty years prior, when my friends were going off to college, I was eagerly planning my wedding and looking forward to life as a stay-at-home mom and homemaker. I never imagined that one day I would be flying across the country to attend an Ivy League executive program with all expenses paid.

Once I faced those fears and settled into my chair, I listened attentively to the professors and began to sit up straighter. Drawing on my real-world entrepreneurial experience, I realized I had important value to add to the lectures in this academic environment, so I engaged in my classes and offered my feedback on what was taught. I may not have a bachelor's or master's degree, but at that moment, I realized it didn't matter. I belonged here.

My doubt was replaced with self-confidence and I felt compassion for my heart and mind for the mental exhaustion I had put myself through leading up to this program.

Over the past 27 years of building my career—growing from a bank teller, to a solo financial advisor, to now CEO of my wealth management firm—I have found myself experiencing many pivotal moments of holding two opposing beliefs. For example, I want to hire a new rockstar team member, but I also want my firm to hit our profit goal. I personally want to pay off a debt, but I also want to buy a new home on the lake. I want to save and invest for the future, but I also want to go shopping and get a new outfit for that event that's next week.

This might be how you feel as you read this book and it's okay and completely normal to feel two opposing emotions or beliefs when it comes to such an important topic as money. I encourage you to lean into this and hold space for both.

My success came from constantly bouncing between my safe comfort zone and being willing to feel and face my fears; or walk into the room I didn't believe I belonged; or invest in myself, my business, and others. And do you know what? Doing this works. In some moments you may not feel like it works—I know I didn't at times—but if you are willing to engage, be courageous, and welcome the feedback, the feedback leads to trusting yourself.

I have written this book to be different from other money books out there. I won't be using fear, shame, or a scarcity mentality to try to change your behaviors and push you toward your goals. Those tactics only work in the short term and the motivation will wane. Instead, I want this book to have a long-lasting impact on your financial aspirations that inspire you to change your life.

Because you picked up and are reading this book, I have faith that you want to experience the change it can bring to your life, specifically around money. No matter what your experience has been with money, I know that it can be even better.

Below are just a few of the results that you can receive from reading this book as you unpack your beliefs around money and learn all of the Money Loves You tools.

- Transform your relationship with money.
- Shatter conventional rules and trust yourself to know what is right for your situation.
- Overcome what holds you back with your money.
- Money becomes simple.
- Implement a strategy for your money and build wealth on your terms.
- Experience financial freedom, feel inspired, and create lasting momentum to maximize your wealth.
- Be an example to your family and community so they can create financial freedom and independence.

You might be here because you want more—more time, more money, more freedom, more of life's experiences—without the hustle. It could be that you desire a different relationship with money or to possibly break through the beliefs around money that keep you stuck. Often, I hear from my clients that they can make a lot of money but have a hard time keeping it and turning it into wealth.

What exactly is wealth? Wealth means different things to all of us. Some will say wealth is purely monetary, but I believe it extends beyond money. To me, wealth is, yes, money and resources but also a feeling, a state of being; it's about having the freedom to make choices for you and your family in regards to your health, social life, career, experiences, and living out your life's purpose. It's the ability to make decisions based on what you want to do rather than on what you can afford to do. The power lies within you to define what wealth means to you. And that's what I am inviting you to do in this book.

I am excited to guide you through all of these possibilities, to teach you the ways that have worked for me for years, and to partner with you to help facilitate your transformation. I know you, just like many others, can experience big change.

For whatever reason you have found yourself here, I am honored to be on this journey with you and thrilled for your future. No matter where you have been or what your money story is, there is a way forward and a new level of abundance to find. There is light at the end of your tunnel, and I promise you—you are not in a cave! I've got you and we are going on this journey together to create an even better relationship between you and your money.

I believe *money does love you* and as you read on, we will unpack this concept together.

CHAPTER ONE

CAN MONEY LOVE?

Money can take on many forms. It can be a coin, a piece of paper, a concept, or a number on a screen. Money is also energy through an exchange of value which provides the experiences and things we need and desire. Money, at its most fundamental definition, is a resource. It is as available and abundant to you as the air you breathe.

So, can money, this abundant resource and energy, really love you? How is this? Money doesn't have emotions. It's not a person. It is just money. Yes, it is *just money* and we all have a personal relationship with money, whether we recognize it or not. Embodying the concept of *money loves you* is simply a powerful personification that teaches us that we are in charge of how money exists in our lives.

Money does not hold power over you. Who you are is what money will be for you. The idea behind *Money Loves You* is that money is like a mirror that will reflect whatever you give it—the stories, the beliefs (positive or negative)—and it will magnify those things in the mirror back to you. This is great if you have a positive relationship with money, but it can be challenging if you don't.

My hope is that you will learn, if you haven't already, how to truly, deeply, and unconditionally love yourself. When you love you, money will love you because money is an amplifier. If you are a generous and cheerful giver, money will flow back to you. If you restrict and hold on tightly, your money will be restricted. If you are responsible and make wise decisions, your investments will be solid. If you are a high-risk taker and invest rashly, then expect to lose money. When you amplify love, you amplify your money.

Once you master these mindsets and principles and consistently apply the frameworks in this book, everything about your money will take care of itself. Money becomes simply a resource. It becomes a non-issue because you've risen above it, you've mastered it. When someone conquers emotional eating, they are no longer tied to the need for food to replace self-love, self-compassion, self-trust. The same is true with money.

When we think of our experiences with money, more times than not those thoughts make us feel ashamed and trigger emotions of guilt, regret, and resentment.

These negative emotions over time can lead to a lack or scarcity mentality with our money. "Money" can create anxiety and worry over not having enough. Or, if you have a lot of it, "money" can create in you an overwhelming fear of being judged, or it can create a burden of how to manage money in a responsible way.

Our relationship with money is either created by default or intentionally learned at some point in life. The good news is: it's never too early or too late to start having a positive relationship with money.

Our conditioning happens from a young age. Growing up, we witnessed our parents, grandparents, and other caregivers deal with and talk about money. This could have been positive or negative. Did you witness your parents argue about money? Did you hear, "we don't have enough money," "you can't have that," or "we can't afford this"? Maybe "money is the root of all evil," or possibly there was silence and money was never a topic of conversation . . . ever.

You could be a lucky one who experienced parents with a healthy mindset around money, which leads to either a strong financial foundation or potentially rebellious mindset, thinking *I don't need to be smart with money; my parents have enough and I will inherit it one day.*

CAN MONEY LOVE?

Did you hear, "we have enough," or "we save and invest our money"? Did they teach you the importance of saving, investing, and using debt wisely? I find this rarely to be the case, but fortunately for me, it was my story.

My first job outside of babysitting was flipping burgers at McDonald's when I was 17 and I made $5.00 an hour. I remember my first raise a couple months after I started working: it was 10 cents and I was so excited to earn that money. Shortly after receiving my first couple of paychecks and after spending money on a new outfit and tickets to go see a New Kids on the Block concert, my dad talked to me about saving and investing. He set me up with my very first mutual fund and I remember writing out a check for $25 to send to that fund. A mutual fund is like a big pot of money collected from many people, and a professional manager uses that money to buy a group of different stocks, bonds, or other investments to help everyone's money grow.

Each time I would send in a check, the company would send me a statement with a coupon attached to it and that encouraged me to send in more money. That began a habit of investing monthly, a habit I still have today. That also got me interested in stocks and investing, which led to my career.

Looking back now, I realize what a gift my dad gave me. I also see, after helping thousands of people with their money and investing, how rare that interaction was. I am blessed to have parents and grandparents who had healthy money habits and who wanted to share that advice and wisdom with me.

Most school curricula don't include teaching students about money, and I know that most of us were not given the basic financial education we needed to make wise financial decisions. When it was time to leave home and start adult life, did you make a plan for your money? Did someone help you, or were you left to your own devices? Did you take on student loan debt or open credit cards at your favorite stores because someone was telling you to do it? Did you hear, "It will help you build credit; it's a good thing"? Unfortunately, these debts lead a lot of people to getting started in life on a weak financial foundation and is a tough place to recover from, but I know recovery is possible.

As a financial advisor on our team, it's a common experience to have clients in their mid-fifties reaching out to us when they just haven't paid much attention to money because they make enough for today and haven't prioritized the future yet. But now, as they get older, they want to grow their wealth, pay less in taxes, and learn how to manage their money better.

At the same time, there is a great wealth transfer happening and new generations are taking over the majority of the wealth. By 2030, Generations X and Y will surpass Baby Boomers in terms of holding the most wealth in the USA.[3] I wonder how many in these next generations feel confident in their abilities to steward this wealth.

There's a saying from Tony Robbins that I repeatedly come back to: "Where focus goes, energy flows."[4] And isn't that the truth? So if money is energy, let's restate this and say: where your focus goes, money flows. The intention of this book is to help you maintain your focus with money until you gain mastery over it.

All too often, and especially with our money goals, we start with a burst of energy, only to lose that spark as our energy goes to competing priorities. But I want you to be constantly fueled by a vision of what lies ahead. I am here to be your guide, to teach you, inspire you, and back you up as you make these big moves ahead with your finances.

And what will be the fuel that keeps your vision of the future alive? Love. This book is about creating a loving relationship with money, which starts with a loving relationship with yourself. When you understand that you are loved just as you are and can love yourself just as you are, you begin to see that you have everything you need to become financially healthy and able to create a life of wealth and freedom. Then you will feel empowered to release any shame or fear that has blocked you from refueling and continuing into the future you desire. Attaining the future you envision is possible.

Disclosures:

[3] *Cerulli Associates. "U.S. High-Net-Worth and Ultra-High-Net-Worth Markets 2023." https://www.cerulli.com/reports/us-high-net-worth-and-ultra-high-net-worth-markets-2021, accessed December 22, 2023.*

[4] *Anthony Robbins, X (formerly Twitter). June 12, 2022, 9:23 a.m., https://twitter.com/TonyRobbins/status/1536370347555309281?lang=en, accessed December 22, 2023.*

Money Loves You Mindset Principle

Embodying the concept of Money Loves You is simply a powerful personification that teaches us that we are in charge of how money exists in our life.

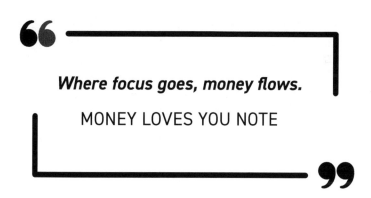

Where focus goes, money flows.

MONEY LOVES YOU NOTE

CHAPTER TWO

IT IS ALL POSSIBLE

Love is always the answer, even with our money. This statement may sound lofty and unrealistic to you, but no matter what financial decisions or challenges we face in life, approaching them with love, compassion, and care is the best way to handle them. With this lens, we can gain a new perspective on money matters and prioritize being kind and loving to ourselves and our partners.

Let's explore the future that is possible with your money. We will not do this through fear, shame, worry, OR budgeting—that is the old way. If you have read books on managing money, these old tactics are used to push you toward your goal. Fear, shame, or guilt might work for short-term results, but ultimately, they leave you feeling defeated and you will find yourself back in your old money patterns that don't work.

There will be times of stress—especially when we are dealing with money—and none of us can escape this. When you are triggered and feeling negative emotions, it is important to remember to pause and acknowledge what you are feeling and bring awareness to it. Doing this will help you step out of the chaos and into intention.

When we are feeling overwhelmed or stuck, it's hard—and often terrifying—to zoom out and see the bigger picture. When things aren't going the way you expect, it's hard to envision a different future. I want to encourage you, offer you hope, and provide a path to creating a better relationship with money. Whether you have made your share of money mistakes, been mediocre with your finances, or are already financially independent, there are always areas in which to improve.

There is a different way, and we don't know what we don't know. The negative feelings and words we use toward ourselves or our partners in moments of despair rarely help to motivate us. Feelings of guilt lead to shame, disappointment, and worry, which then lead to fear and resentment. These are not emotions we want to be trapped in. It's normal and natural to feel these emotions, especially when things go wrong. The sooner we can transform despair into hope, the sooner we can begin to take charge of our future.

When we feel negative emotions, it's easy for the momentum to take us down. What if we acknowledge how we are feeling, deal with our money triggers and limiting beliefs (which we will dive into in Chapter 7), and then make a plan to move ourselves out of negativity and into momentum with hope, faith, and love? Shifting our relationship with money is possible and knowing how to make this shift opens the way to move out of money overwhelm and into money empowerment.

We all will know periods of turmoil, heartache, pain, and regret. The secret to financial success is how we use these times for our good and create a path back to abundance. Our pasts can serve as energy and fuel for the future we crave. As humans, we are resilient, and there is always a way forward.

I felt like I grew up fast when I got married at 19, with plans to follow in my mother's footsteps and be an amazing stay-at-home mom. At the same time, I went to work for a local bank for something to do and fell in love with helping others with their finances.

During the next few years, my young marriage faced major challenges and I was struggling big-time. We were unsuccessful in getting pregnant and were dealing with the issues of a codependent relationship. At 19, it's hard to know who you are and what you want in life, let alone trying to navigate being in a marriage. I didn't feel like I could make my own decisions because I had little money of my own; my husband made the majority of our household income, which made me subconsciously feel trapped. I had to do something to gain financial independence.

By age 23, I had all my securities licenses, a few years of experience, and I really wanted to *be* a financial advisor rather than support one. I went to the program manager and said, "I am ready to be an advisor," and she responded that as soon as the current advisor left, I could have that position. Well, if I would have waited, that would not have happened for another 10 years!

Realizing I had hit the glass ceiling, feeling both frustrated and bulletproof, I left the bank in 2001 and started my own business—what is now Financial Freedom Wealth Management Group. The financial services industry was approximately 85% male-dominated and my chances of success would have appeared slim from the outside. Who is going to trust a 6-foot, blonde, 20-something woman with their millions of dollars?

These needs to make my own money and prove myself worthy ignited a fierce drive in me for independence, and I had a lot to prove to the world. I invested all my time and energy into the business. I loved the work and helping others. It gave me a sense of satisfaction and made me feel important. It also provided an escape and distraction from my personal life.

My desire to be financially independent transformed me into wanting that independence for others. This desire was stronger than my doubts and fears—my constant companions. Thankfully, I had a few mentors in my life who believed in me and inspired me to keep going when the valleys got deep. The difficult personal experiences early on in my adulthood planted in my subconscious a limiting belief of unworthiness and strong feelings that I was not good enough. Those beliefs are what drove my behaviors for the next 12 years.

I was on a chase for feeling "good enough," and I temporarily received my "high" from the success. An average week for me was filled with 30 client appointments, catching up on emails after or during dinner, and then doing paperwork until midnight. I was addicted to "doing" because it allowed me to feel in control and have my own money to do all the things I wanted—to go shopping, invest in myself, travel and explore—to feel independent and free.

When I was able to truly give up control and learn how to receive (more on this in Chapter 5), I was able to escape the chase, the constant hustle for more, and the need to prove myself worthy. Letting go has brought even more money into my life but more importantly, it's brought peace and true freedom—the things I was subconsciously longing for all along.

I no longer strive for more money. I am now inspired by the person I am becoming: a woman who is able to provide transformation through contribution, impact, and growth.

This was my journey. I can now see the reasons for the things I did and connect the dots. My obsessive drive and ambition got me through some hard times and are what I needed to get me where I am today, but it's no longer where I get my self-worth. We are all entirely worthy (more on this in Chapter 10).

I am writing this book because I strongly desire this for others: to help you let go of the hustle and surrender to what can come into your life by shifting your beliefs and identity.

What type of relationship do you want with money? What do you want money to do for you? What does money mean to you? Do you hate money because it causes stress, anxiety, or arguments with your partner? Or is it a tool and a power assist, a "partner" that helps your dreams come true?

In my experience, I have found that money mirrors how we feel about ourselves—we attract that which we are in the world—so money matches our generosity, our ability to invest in ourselves, our ability to give and receive, and our ability to trust ourselves and others, all of which point to loving ourselves.

Money loves you when you love you.

I know this is a big statement and it is intentionally open for you to interpret how it best serves you, but let me unpack my intention behind it. When you love yourself, you are kind and compassionate with yourself and you accept who you are, your past, and even the mistakes you've made.

I have a strong belief and faith in God and I know my relationship with God is rooted in unconditional love. This means there is nothing I could ever do to gain love or lose love. No matter what your personal beliefs are, I believe you're able to be loved unconditionally. My aim is to love myself and others with this kind of love. This love is compassionate, joyful, enduring, gentle, and generous.

Throughout my career I have seen it all when it comes to money disasters: hundreds of thousands of dollars in credit card and consumer debt with very little income; bankruptcy; spending millions of inheritance in very little time; investing everything in one stock and then losing it all as the company declared bankruptcy. Nothing shocks me. I am holding space for all the mess ups and failures of your past and I extend unconditional love to you.

When we can embrace and love ourselves unconditionally by extending grace and forgiveness for our mishaps and troubles, we can see the bigger picture and let our experiences ignite a different path forward. We can have faith that our past doesn't dictate our future but actually can be the very thing that equips us to know that everything is unfolding perfectly and happening for our greater good.

It's possible to feel excited about your relationship with money and know that you can experience amazing things by having a healthy money mindset and being empowered with having money.

I want to get this out of the way in the beginning:

This book isn't about loving money or becoming obsessed with money.

The belief that money is the root of all evil is a common misconception. This saying is often misquoted from the Bible. The actual biblical verse is from 1 Timothy 6:10, which states, "For the love of money is a root of all kinds of evil" (New International Version, or NIV). The key distinction here is that it's not money itself that is considered evil, but the excessive *love or attachment to money* that can lead to unethical and harmful behavior. The root of ethical or unethical behavior lies in human intentions, values, and choices, not in money itself.

The Bible has many insights about money that we can glean wisdom from and no matter what your faith is or isn't, we can learn from its principles. I am reminded of the parable of the talents from the Bible in Matthew 25:14–30 which can be paraphrased and goes something as follows.

A wealthy man prepared to go on a journey, and before leaving, he entrusted his wealth to his servants. To one servant, he gave five portions, to another two, and to the last one, he gave one portion—each according to their abilities.

The first servant invested the five portions and gained five more. The second servant invested the two portions and gained two more. However, the third servant, fearing loss, buried his one portion in the ground.

After a time, the wealthy man returned and evaluated his servants' efforts. He praised the first two servants for their diligence and entrusted them with even more responsibilities. But he reprimanded the third servant for not using his portion wisely.

The parable teaches that those who use their talents effectively will be rewarded, while those who fearfully hold back will miss out on the opportunities presented to them.

We can interpret this story from two distinct perspectives. First, it's referring to talents that are our God-given abilities or gifts that only we possess, and it's our life's purpose to bring to the world. And second, it refers to actual money we are blessed to receive. It clearly provides us with a principle that neither money nor our natural abilities are meant to be dormant. We and our money are meant for more—for taking action, for investing, for creating memories. Let us not waste our gifts or our money!

You are always your *best* investment and should therefore be your *first* investment. I have so much proof of this in my own life.

In 2009, I moved to a new broker-dealer with a dream to build my own independent financial advisory firm. I went from being a solo advisor with a great support system to feeling alone. With my dream alive but no idea how to achieve it, I knew I needed help. Out of nowhere appeared an opportunity for me to join a coaching program specifically designed to help solo financial advisors build a million-dollar business. The only catch was that it cost $13,000.

At the time, my gross revenue was only $100,000. I felt so strongly that it was the right investment to make, but I was equally freaked out at the cost of it.

Without telling anyone, I committed to it and it turned out to be one of my early lessons in trusting myself.

IT IS ALL POSSIBLE

I learned a lot in that program and met people who mentored me to build a million-dollar business. It also led me down the path to hiring and building an amazing team at Financial Freedom Wealth Management Group. Today, we help over 1,600 individuals, families, and business owners pursue their dreams and financial freedom.

Clients are often shocked to hear me say, "yes, invest in that business coach," or "yes, take your family on that vacation and pay for it all." Buy a new car, spend money on your home remodel—money is meant to be used! Money is a resource to be utilized and invested in experiences that create lifelong memories. I have found this brings the best of returns.

Money is meant to be given and received; it's meant to flow. *It's energy, it's currency, it's meant to be in motion and when it's in motion, it creates momentum. Money loves momentum.*

"Money loves you" is a fun-loving comment I have found myself saying to my clients, my friends, and even to myself. I often see a smile come across a friend's face when I say, "Remember, money loves you!"

No matter where you are on your journey toward creating, growing, or maintaining your wealth, I want you to know that all I have shared with you is possible! I have seen it over and over with my clients and in my own life. You can do this.

All of your dreams and aspirations can come to you.

Money Loves you Mindset Principle

Money mirrors how you feel about yourself—
we attract that which we are in the world.

Money loves you when you love you.

Money is meant to flow.

> *Love is always the answer, even with our money.*
>
> MONEY LOVES YOU NOTE

CHAPTER THREE

PREPARE FOR GROWTH

Allowing money to love you and amplify who you are is totally possible for you. I strongly believe this and have no doubt it is true for you. But, a strong tree won't grow if the roots are rotted. For a lot of us, this means we have to go back and examine our financial foundations; we have to get to the root of the issues we have with money, even if the roots are rotted.

In this chapter, we are going to begin by examining your money roots. We do this by looking at your thoughts, feelings, and beliefs around money, because right now, THEY could be blocking the flow of money or keeping you stuck.

This can feel tricky since it's always hard to see our own beliefs because they always feel TRUE to us. The easiest way to begin to see our own money lies is by seeing them through others and their stories.

Join me as I share a few stories from people just like you. I invite you to find yourself in these stories. See THEIR money lies, and begin to notice where their story might look like your story.

Money Maker

Do you find yourself saying, "I can make a lot of money, but I just can't seem to hold onto it"? First, you are not alone and second, congrats, money loves you! I'd love to tell you a story about Suzy.

Suzy is a successful solo entrepreneur and can easily make money. In fact, she has cash flows of $50,000–60,000 a month, covers her business expenses, and pays herself a consistent salary. She enjoys nice things, loves to take her family out to dinner, and plans a couple vacations each year. At the end of the year she looks back at her results and wonders what she has to show for her success and hard work.

Over time this pattern has led her to thinking, *I am not making progress, I can't keep my money, every month I work so hard to make the money, and I am so tired. Where does all the money go? Why did I have to pay so much in taxes? It just doesn't make sense. Money is so hard.* This leaves her feeling frustrated, stressed, and overwhelmed. Her belief, which has become her identity, is: I have to keep doing and giving just to make enough to survive. In fact, with some self-reflection, she discovers her self-worth is derived from the hustle and making money. *How am I ever going to change? I am never going to be able to retire. I'll die working. Is it all worth it?*

Do you see yourself in her story? Are these thoughts familiar to you?

Empty Nester

The kids have successfully transitioned to adulthood and they are making lives for themselves. Give yourself a pat on the back, as I know this isn't an easy task.

Let me introduce you to Mike and Linda. They are 55 and 52 (respectively) and with all the kids out of the house, it is finally time to look ahead and live the life they have been dreaming about. They can spend money on themselves, take those dreamy "couple" vacations, and finally put money away for retirement.

Where do they start? It has always been about the kids and they have never learned how to save and invest correctly for their future. Early in their marriage, Mike invested $10,000 in a company his brother-in-law recommended and he lost all their money. This contributed to a lack of trust in Mike and Linda's relationship because Mike didn't tell Linda about the investment and she found out about it at the family Thanksgiving dinner the following year. How could he have hidden this from her?

Linda doesn't want to make another mistake and thinks that they will lose money again if they invest in the stock market. She still carries resentment toward Mike for not talking to her before making that failed investment. Mike knows that he made a wrong decision early on with the stock and feels regret about it. He also feels defeated and doesn't know how to rebuild Linda's trust around investing.

Does anything in this story resonate with you?

Instant Wealth

The inheritance check is in the mail from the attorney's office. You're thinking about how you will handle this new money.

I want to share about Ben and Jane. The past couple of years have been rough. Two years ago, Ben's dad died from a major heart attack and his mom passed away nine months ago. Ben and Jane have never felt so many emotions: grief for his parents' deaths, excitement that $1.1 million is heading their way, and fear of doing the wrong thing with their money.

When the check arrives, they deposit it into their bank savings account. They want to be careful to not do anything too risky with this amount of money. They decide that with a part of the money they will buy a new car. After all, they deserve to have a sports car now that the kids are out of the house. Next, Jane notices that a salon down the street has a for sale sign in the window, and for years she has dreamed of owning her own salon. She talks to Ben and feels this is the perfect time to do it. "We can use the funds from your parents," she states. "They would be so proud of me."

After a year passes they look at their bank balance and see only $700,000. "How did that happen?" Ben asks. Jane explains that taking over at the salon had more expenses than she had planned. She adds, "And remember, with me working six days a week, we needed that two-week luxury vacation in Hawaii."

Ben shares his dad's love for food and is a master chef. After they received the inheritance, he decided to quit the restaurant, stay home, and prepare meals for Jane, which she *needed* after a long day at the salon. He decides he deserves a kitchen remodel and invests over $250,000 into their home. "Our home is a great investment," he shares with Jane.

Another year passes and they now have less than $300,000 in their bank savings. "I can't believe it's almost gone," Ben tells Jane one evening. "We lived off so little before they died. How did we go through so much money? I thought the money could never run out. I thought this was our chance to get set up for life."

Have you received an unexpected amount of money, only to later find it dwindled?

Suddenly Single

You just experienced the worst day of your life: Your favorite person in the world, the love of your life, has died. And you are left suddenly single. Alone is the toughest place to be after building a lifetime with your partner. I have witnessed this with clients so many times over my career.

Melissa called me just days after Larry died unexpectedly. Tears flowed as she shared with me the final moments of his life. "I am here for you. You will get through this. You are strong and smart and you can do this," I console her. "I'm not," she states. "I can't do this. He dealt with all the finances and I don't even know where to start. He always took care of everything. I'm not smart enough. I don't even know where all the money is and I don't understand these investments. I can't keep track of all of this. It's so confusing."

Have you lost a loved one and felt this despair?

Never the Right Time

Many families have competing priorities over their finances and have a hectic life. Let's take a peek into the life of Peter and Andrea.

By their early forties, Peter and Andrea had been married for 15 years and they both worked full time. Their two children, Sidney and Mike, were in 8th and 6th grade and active in sports. Sidney also had a horse and was in 4H. It seemed as if every night and weekend was taken up with sport practice or games, or attending to the horse chores.

Peter and Andrea met with a financial advisor to set up a plan, but after that initial meeting they felt the timing wasn't right to start and canceled their second meeting. They never got around to creating that financial plan. By the time the kids started looking at colleges, Peter and Andrea realized they had only $25,000 in their retirement accounts and nothing saved for their kids' college. The kids will have to take out student loans for their education.

Peter and Andrea can't believe how fast time went by and regret not starting to pay attention to their money earlier in life. Even though they felt the timing wasn't right, they didn't intend for all those years to go by without any focus on their money.

Can you relate to a busy life and not making money a priority?

Parting of Ways

Currently, 40–50% of marriages in America end in divorce. That means that 40–50% of you reading this book may have found yourself in a completely new life and financial situation. Your story might look different than the one below, but let me tell you about Betsy.

After 17 years of marriage and having three kids, Betsy finds herself holding the official divorce papers in her hands. She never imagined that she would be single once again at the age of 43. She knew it would be hard to be a single mother. Betsy expected the lonely nights, and the random outbursts of tears as she drives down the road. But what she didn't anticipate is the overwhelming weight and stress of being the sole financial provider for her and her three children.

Luckily, she had started a small business a few years before her divorce, but up until this point, she had funneled all of her earnings back into her business. Betsy now has to figure out how to continue running her business and learn how to double her income, all while going through the challenges of being a single mother. At times, she finds herself walking down the hallway of her home asking herself why she thought she could do this. Oftentimes, she questions her ability to manage all the bills while trying to expand her business to create more income. Many nights she has fallen asleep feeling guilty for not making enough money. When her children came home with ripped shoes, she found herself not wanting to buy them new shoes out of fear that there wouldn't be enough money to pay the bills. She feels like she holds the weight of the world on her shoulders.

Have you been through a situation like this or something similar? What part of this story can you relate to?

Everyone has their own money story—a story that has impacted their thoughts and actions around money. Now that you have read a few stories and witnessed the thoughts of the people in the stories, I want to help you uncover the stories that you have.

I have a thoughtful exercise that will help you start playing around with potential issues and help you get to the root cause of those issues. In the illustration of this beautiful tree below, I want you to write in the leaves of the tree some feelings, thoughts, behaviors, or stories that you have connected to money.

If you are still having trouble, ask yourself: what is my earliest memory with money? What do I remember learning about money as a child or young adult? What do I find myself thinking or feeling about money?

Next, as you reflect on what you have written on the leaves, recognize these as symptoms but likely not the root cause of the belief. On the exposed roots, write your thoughts on what you might believe or think to be the cause of the symptoms or the rot.

For example, I ignore my finances (symptom), and the root of the issue is a belief that I am not smart enough.

PREPARE FOR GROWTH

Illustration by Jeff Skirvin

We began this chapter talking about clearing out any "rot" that is within the roots of your financial tree. I shared with you some stories so you could hear your own inner thoughts. By doing so, hopefully you are becoming aware of what has been holding you back from the success that is completely available to you.

When we uncover what is holding us back, we create room for new perspectives and new energies to come in. New perspectives can bring fresh soil to our roots and new energies can give us hope for a better future.

Money Loves You Mindset Principle

Allowing money to love you and amplify who
you are is totally possible for you.

When we uncover what is holding us back, we create
room for new perspectives and new energies to come in.

Money meets you where you are.

MONEY LOVES YOU NOTE

CHAPTER FOUR

UNDERSTANDING THE CONSCIOUS, SUBCONSCIOUS, AND SUPERCONSCIOUS MIND

Now that you are beginning to see how your thoughts and beliefs around money are affecting your results with money, it is time to learn how to rewire those thoughts. It can also be an opportunity to tap into the superpower of your mind that will be the power to assist in generating exactly what you want. But to do this, it's important to understand how your brilliant mind works (yes, your mind is brilliant!).

I like to think about the mind as having three distinct parts: the conscious, subconscious, and superconscious. All three are powerful in equipping and empowering your relationship with money.

Imagine your mind is like an iceberg. The part you can see above the water is your conscious mind. It's where you think, make decisions, and solve problems.

Now, below the water there's a hidden part called the subconscious mind and just like an iceberg, it has way more capacity than the conscious mind.

It holds all your memories, feelings, beliefs, and habits—though you may not be not aware of them.

But there's one more part that is rarely referenced. It's the superconscious mind, which is like the tip of the iceberg that reaches for the sky. It's your higher self, the part of your mind that's connected to something bigger than just you. It's where you find your intuition, creativity, and a sense of purpose. It's like a wise loved one guiding you to make good choices and discover your true potential. Let's explore these in more detail.

Conscious Mind

The conscious mind is all the things in our awareness and what we are thinking about in the present. It's developed through all our perspectives in life including experiences, learnings, wishes, feelings, and thinking.

With the conscious mind we can think logically, rationalize, make plans, and form judgements. It is also where our willpower lives. The conscious mind is unknowingly running automatic programs from the subscious mind.

Here is an example of how the conscious mind works.

Story of the Conscious Mind

I want to introduce you to Lily, a self-aware woman who knows the importance of taking care of her money. Lily's parents taught her about money and the importance of making smart financial decisions. As an adult, Lily has continued to learn all she can about money and enjoys working with a financial advisor to guide her. She reads, asks questions, and feels empowered with her money.

Lily's dream is to own a beautiful home in the country with land for her horses to roam. In her early thirties, Lily started saving money specifically for this dream. After a few years, a property came up for sale and it was perfect. Lily looked at the property with her realtor, but it was priced just over the amount she could afford.

After talking over the costs with her financial advisor and coach, Lily made the hard decision to wait until she saved more funds so she could comfortably pay for a home. She decided having a bigger mortgage was not worth the stress and worry it would cause. Lily knows herself and although

UNDERSTANDING THE CONSCIOUS, SUBCONSCIOUS, AND SUPERCONSCIOUS MIND

she would feel disappointed about not getting this dream home now, she loved herself first and made a decision her future self would thank her for.

Just like a loving guide, Lily's story shows us that when we take time to think clearly, seek wise counsel, and consider what is in our long-term best interest, we can make decisions with our money that are right for our path.

Subconscious Mind

The subconscious mind is a powerful part of the mind that makes decisions without us having to actively think about them. The subconscious mind is working 24-hours a day and keeps the score of all our emotions and feelings.

We are not fully aware of the subconscious mind and this is what makes things tricky. Based on our programming, we make choices that sabotage progress or hold ourselves back from something we desire because of a limiting belief held in the subconscious mind. If we are not aware of our subconscious, it often holds power over us and influences all sorts of our behaviors in the present.

This is why digging into the subconscious mind and examining behaviors and beliefs that are not favorable to us allows us to understand our programming. It is possible to explore our subconscious, reveal where our beliefs came from, and then edit them to improve our future. This process is incredibly liberating and really allows us to break free from limiting beliefs and go after whatever we desire (see the step-by-step guide in Chapter 7).

Catching ourselves in a reactive mode, then pausing to observe and examine our behaviors, allows us to transform and act in alignment with what we desire both now and for our future self.

Here is an example of the subconscious mind and how it affects your life.

Story of the Subconscious Mind

In a quaint little town there lived a boy named Alex. He was like any other sixth-grader: enjoying soccer games with friends, exploring the woods nearby, and harboring dreams about his future. However, what made Alex different from his peers were his subconscious beliefs about money, shaped by his father's views.

Alex's father, Mr. Johnson, had a lifelong struggle with financial matters. His constant worries about bills, debts, and the cost of living were daily conversations in their home. These discussions inadvertently left their mark on Alex. Without even realizing it, Alex started developing limiting beliefs about money. He began to think that money was hard to come by, that it required immense effort to earn, and that it could never be truly enough.

One sunny Saturday morning while playing soccer with his friends at the local park, Alex overheard their conversations about what they wanted to be when they grew up. Some wanted to become astronauts, doctors, or famous musicians. Alex's dream was to become a marine biologist because he loved the ocean and all the cool stuff in it. But then he had a sad thought: *I might never have enough money for all the things I need to learn and do.*

Unconsciously, this learned limiting belief started to affect various aspects of Alex's life. He hesitated to ask his parents for money for school supplies, fearing it might strain their finances. He avoided joining sports and club activities because he believed they would cost too much and he didn't want to burden his family with what he wanted.

One day, Alex decided to talk to his dad about it. "Dad," he asked, "why do you always seem so worried about money?"

His father paused, taken aback by the question, and then smiled warmly. "Well, Alex, I guess I've let my concerns about money affect how I talk about it. I want the best for our family, and sometimes that concern takes over. Don't you worry, we will be okay."

Though Alex felt a bit relieved, his subconscious beliefs about money continued to influence him. As he grew older, Alex encountered numerous challenges that his limiting beliefs made even more challenging. His dream of becoming a marine biologist remained elusive, and he missed out on opportunities because of his subconscious doubts about money.

The story of Alex teaches us that sometimes, our subconscious beliefs about money can indeed hold us back and it's not our fault. I think it's why people give up on their dreams so easily. The power to overcome these beliefs remains within Alex's reach, waiting for the day he realizes that his beliefs need to be exposed and transformed.

UNDERSTANDING THE CONSCIOUS, SUBCONSCIOUS, AND SUPERCONSCIOUS MIND

Superconscious Mind

I believe the superconscious mind is a higher, spiritual aspect of consciousness. When we align with our higher selves—the part of the mind that knows the truth—we can access the part of the mind that is connected to divine wisdom and guidance. When we access and align with our superconscious through faith, prayer, and meditation, we can overcome challenges, attract what we desire, and experience personal transformation and miracles. It really is our superhero.

It's the version of you that always knows *your* truth, not everyone else's truth. It knows no judgment or fear and offers only unconditional love to you and your subconscious. When you learn how to tap into the superconscious mind and connect with the Divine, you will activate one of your greatest abilities of creation and manifest amazing things in your life.

Your superconscious mind is like an extraordinary partner or a supportive helper, giving you ideas and insights to help you become your best self and make the world a better place. It's always working for your good.

Here is an example of how the superconscious mind can be used in your life.

Story of the Superconscious Mind

Sarah owned a small bakery called Sweet Delights, on the East Coast. Sarah had always been passionate about baking, and her dream was to turn her little bakery into a thriving business when the kids went off to college.

One day, Sarah faced a tough decision. She had the opportunity to expand her bakery by opening a second location in a nearby town. Her current location was profitable and her business was going well, but opening a second location would be a financial risk and she wasn't sure if she should go for it. Sarah didn't want to make the wrong choice and this was new territory for her.

That night, as Sarah lay in bed, she closed her eyes and tried to clear her mind. She put her hand on her heart and took a few deep breaths as she prayed for direction and clarity for a decision. As she lay still she heard a gentle voice within her.

"Sarah," she sensed the voice inside her, "I know you're worried, but you've worked so hard to build your bakery. Expanding will bring more customers and make your dream come true. Go for it."

Sarah felt a sense of comfort and clarity wash over her. She couldn't explain it, but she knew that her superconscious mind, connected to the Divine, was giving her the insight she was asking for. She decided to take the leap and open the second bakery.

As the new bakery opened its doors, customers from the neighborhood flooded in and Sweet Delights became even more popular. The extra income helped Sarah not only cover the costs of the new location but also invest in new recipes and hire additional staff, plus pay the college tuition for her two sons. Her business started to grow like never before.

One day, a food critic from a popular magazine visited Sweet Delights. Sarah's heart raced as she awaited the critic's review. She knew it could be a game-changer for her business.

Once again, Sarah turned to prayer for guidance. She heard the whisper, "Believe in your skills, Sarah. You've put your heart and soul into your bakery."

The critic's review came out, and it was glowing! Sweet Delights received five stars. People from all over the city flocked to Sarah's bakeries. Her dream of turning her small bakery into a successful business had come true.

Over the years, Sarah continued to listen to her superconscious mind—her still small voice within. She learned that the more she created a relationship with it, the more she could access it and hear the guidance. Even though she was busy, she took time daily to be in prayer and reflection, either by taking a walk in nature or finding a quiet time to be by herself. This grounded her and she made smart financial choices, expanded her business even further, and secured a bright future for herself and her family.

Sarah's story became an inspiration to others in the city, teaching them that with hard work, a bit of risk, and a trust in their inner wisdom connected to the Divine, they could make their dreams come true. Sarah's faith had been her guiding star on her financial journey, proving that it was there to help her make choices that lead to success and prosperity.

UNDERSTANDING THE CONSCIOUS, SUBCONSCIOUS, AND SUPERCONSCIOUS MIND

As you begin to understand these three areas of your mind, you will see how this understanding unlocks your much-desired freedom. In the next few chapters, you will learn how to examine your behaviors in a healthy way without judgment.

You will uncover those limiting beliefs and self-sabotaging actions that have been hijacking your success and then learn how to remove them from your life. When you begin to see how your limiting thoughts are sabotaging your financial success, you will be primed for true transformation.

Your transformation is essential for you to move to the next level with your money success. Are you ready to let go, receive, and have a full transformation with your money?

Money Loves You Mindset Principle

When you can learn how to tap into the superconscious mind and connect with the Divine, you will activate one of your greatest abilities of creation and manifest amazing things in your life.

Developing a healthy relationship with money is critical. You can't be wealthy by ignoring your money.

MONEY LOVES YOU NOTE

CHAPTER FIVE

READY TO RECEIVE

Have you ever deflected a compliment from someone? Your partner says, "Wow, you look beautiful (or handsome) today." What is your first response? Be honest. . . . Do you say, "No I don't" or maybe downplay it and feel embarrassed or brush it off? Or do you ignore the compliment and say, "No, you look great." Your response to compliments or acknowledgment and appreciation can provide great insight into your ability to receive.

In childhood, I was taught it is better to give than to receive. A few memory verses that come to mind are: "It is more blessed to give than to receive" (Acts 20:35, NIV) and "God loves a cheerful giver" (2 Cor 9:7, NIV). When I got married, this principle for a successful relationship was shared with us: Give more than you take and your marriage will last.

When I started my business, my mentors encouraged me to give of my time, share my knowledge, and give away services so people would know about me and refer me to their friends. When I started having kids, giving went to the next level. As parents, we would give our kids the world.

Giving is ingrained in our culture and I think it's a crucial part of our human experience, but it's not the only part. It's only half of the equation. We are worthy to receive. "Whatever a man sows, that he will also reap"

(Gal 6:7, New King James Version, or NKJV), meaning that whatever we send out into the world—money or works—will return to us; what we give, we will receive.

Rarely are we encouraged and open to receive; we aren't taught to receive. Why is receiving so hard for us? What blocks us from receiving and, specifically, receiving money? Do we believe it's selfish? Do we believe we don't deserve it? Possibly we don't feel worthy of more. Maybe our shame holds us captive in believing we are not enough, or are undeserving or unloveable. Our subconscious beliefs keep us from being able to receive.

As my business grew and became more successful, the responsibilities also grew and the demands became taxing on me. With three kids under age nine and managing a growing business with increasing demands and serving clients, I was feeling both like I was on top of the world being a superwoman and on the brink of a total breakdown. I didn't realize how burnt out I was until the accident happened.

My oldest daughter, Katelyn, was traveling with my parents and they were hit head-on by a drunk driver. At that same exact time, I was entertaining 40 of my clients on a boat cruise two hours away. I didn't learn about the accident until after I stepped off the boat, looked at my phone, and saw numerous missed calls and frantic text messages. I knew something was terribly wrong. My daughter was being life-flighted to a children's hospital in Portland, Oregon. My assistant drove me to Portland to meet the helicopter and I stayed in the ICU with my daughter for the next week.

I was physically there for her but I found myself needing to juggle the demands of my business from her bedside. I returned phone calls and emails. I placed trades and money-movement orders. I did all the things I felt I needed to do to keep the business going. After all, if I didn't do it as the owner, the business would fall apart—at least, this is what I led myself to believe. I had made myself so relevant, so important in my business that I became the bottleneck. I didn't allow my very capable staff to take over, and they could have. I wasn't open to receiving because I got my value and my worth from doing and giving.

My parents and daughter went on to fully recover, thank you God. I learned a valuable lesson in how to surrender and receive. This was a pivotal moment in my career. If I didn't learn how to delegate and receive help, my business wouldn't be successful. I was forced to surrender control and let go because my strongest desire was to be home that summer to help Katelyn recover.

By not being in the office, I was forced to trust my team. Instead of needing to know all the details (which was really hard for me), I got what was important for me to know. Initially, I felt guilty for not answering calls and emails or being available 24-7. My self-worth came into question as my schedule was cleared and I saw my work addiction. I wasn't free; I was a slave to my business. I did some serious soul-searching that summer as I began to unwind the stories I had told myself for so long and started to detach my sense of worth from the doing.

The feelings of guilt faded as I saw the capabilities of my team expand. I had to step aside and be okay with them doing things their way because the end results were still being met—clients were delighted. The surprising result for me was feeling excited as my team rose to meet the challenges. They felt empowered to embrace these end results as their own, something that I had deprived them of up until this point.

In the weeks and months that followed the accident, I was able to give my staff the gift of trust. While I had *spoken* about trusting my staff (I had hired them after all!), I finally allowed my actions to match my words and let my staff shine. They deserved the spotlight and recognition.

I did not know until after the accident that I was blocking incredible benefits, deeper relationships, and more abundance by using my business and financial success as a source of personal worth. What I actually desired—peace and freedom—I had actually been stopping. I had created a toxic relationship with *having and doing*, whether I knew it or not. I was in a tight-fisted, controlling relationship with my staff, my business, and as a result, my money. Yes, I had become successful financially but at the cost of calm, peace, and the harmony that can only be generated from living a life of love and surrender.

I finally realized what got me to this level of success was not going to take me to the next level. If I wanted to continue to grow a thriving, enduring business, I had to get out of my own way and learn to receive.

When you embrace receiving, you are allowing someone else to give and this creates harmony. This harmony provides exponential benefits with your money, your relationships, and your life.

Letting go of control is part of receiving because when we are giving, we feel in control. As a recovering control freak myself, I know that letting go is complex and challenging. Receiving opens us up to vulnerability and it takes courage to face the truth that we are worthy to receive. Inviting vulnerability allows us to see from a different perspective. See that you are worthy, you are enough, and you can do things differently moving forward.

If receiving a compliment or acknowledgment for a job well-done is something you struggle with, I would encourage you to simply notice your reaction the next time you are showered with praise or a compliment and say, "Thank you." That is it; no defending, no explaining, just simply *thank you*.

Money Loves You Mindset Principle

You are worthy to receive.

When you embrace receiving, you are allowing someone else to give and that creates harmony. This harmony creates exponential benefits with your money, your relationships, and your life.

Letting go of control is part of receiving because when we are giving, we feel in control.

MONEY LOVES YOU NOTE

CHAPTER SIX

TRUST YOURSELF

Early on in my adult life, I was guilty of overspending and not paying attention to our money (because I was the one in charge of it). I would go on shopping sprees and then hide my bags from my husband. When I wore a new outfit he would ask, "Is that new?" I would respond, "Oh, this old thing? No, I have had it forever."

That little white lie felt like no big deal at the time. Looking back now, I know I didn't feel worthy or deserving of spending money on myself. My hubby's reaction to me spending money created guilt and shame in me. I am sure he didn't intend for me to feel that way, but it's how my subconscious interpreted his reaction.

This was a hard habit to break because my behaviors were being driven by subconscious beliefs that were unknown to me at the time.

With more success in my career I found myself looking outside of myself for the answers, asking others what they thought and then allowing their opinions to have more weight than my own. I can now connect this to my once-limiting beliefs that *I am not smart or good enough; they are smarter than me and they know more; and since I don't know what to do, I will follow their direction.* Looking outside for validation or answers points to a limiting belief that *I am not enough.*

Self-trust is an imperative element of self-love. Wise counsel is important; having mentors, advisors, and people you trust for advice is a crucial part of a successful journey. But you want to pay attention when you allow others' advice to override your own inner knowledge.

I have learned from these experiences and failures of not trusting myself and the pain and cost of those experiences. This is one of those lessons that occurred repeatedly until I finally "got it."

I have been following the stock market since high school and investing in stocks since 1995. Through this time there have been bear and bull markets. A bear market happens when prices of many stocks drop by at least 20%, causing an overall downturn in financial markets. This downturn in stock prices makes investors cautious and anxious. In contrast, a bull market is a phase in the stock market when prices of investments are generally rising, and investors are confident, leading to an overall upward trend in financial markets.

During the 2008–09 market downturn, I was at a point where I could invest more money if I chose to do so. My intuition was to go all in with our savings and purchase stocks when they were priced low. However, the news media promoted fear-mongering headlines that put doubt into my mind. Plus, everyone else around me was panicking, so I decided to do a *little* extra investing, but not a lot.

The investments I made during the 2008–09 bear market have contributed significantly to our overall net worth and I am grateful for that. But, I do regret not trusting myself more to go all in. In early 2020 when the pandemic hit and the market fell over 30%, I repeated the same choice I made in the '08–'09 downturn. I knew deep in my gut that I was right. I knew it and I didn't act on it. Twice. TWICE! I could never imagine Chris or my children coming to me and saying, "I have a gut feeling that I am meant to do this" and ignoring them. And then ignoring them again.

My actions, or inactions rather, during the two market downturns taught me more about myself than I anticipated. I have found I must trust myself first and I can only do that if I am seeking the truth—my truth. To seek my truth is to slow down and give myself time devoted to listening and tapping into my superconscious mind. Really listen, like I would Chris or my children. In this case, I am my best teacher, my best advisor, and I gain insights and wisdom when I listen.

I have now learned my lesson and during the next down (or bear) market, I am going all in because I trust myself.

"Whoever can be trusted with very little can also be trusted with much, and whoever is dishonest with very little will also be dishonest with much" (Luke 16:10, NIV). This is a powerful verse in the Bible that gives much insight and wisdom around money and truth. It reminds me of the quote by Martha Beck: "The way we do anything is the way we do everything."[5]

How do we begin to trust ourselves?

It begins by keeping the promises you make to yourself. How often do we say we are going to do something for ourselves and then we don't honor that commitment?

Here is a simple and small exercise to help you to build trust with yourself. I invite you to *commit* to doing something for three days, and then DO it.

Here is a list of activities to consider, but feel free to add your own.

- Walk for 20 minutes every day.
- Journal for 10 minutes a day.
- Sit and do nothing for 5 minutes a day.
- Write down what you spend money on each day.
- _____
- _____

At the end of the three days, acknowledge and celebrate your accomplishments. You did it! You committed to something and you

Disclosures:

[5] Martha Beck, "The Labyrinth of Life," marthabeck.com, March 2013, https://marthabeck.com/2013/03/the-labyrinth-of-life/, accessed December 22, 2023.

finished. This is a simple and powerful way to build trust with yourself and it works.

You may be thinking, "Three days? Big whoop, Julia." Yes, you are right. You may not have climbed Everest, run a marathon (maybe you did!), or revamped your investment portfolio, but you did *something*. And, *something* is different than nothing. *Something* is change. *Something* is your superconscious showing up and saying, "Let's do this!" And, that *something*—that change—is the birthplace of confidence.

Trusting ourselves requires confidence. What I have learned about confidence is, it doesn't arrive until you make new decisions and take action. Many want confidence before taking action, but in reality, you must take action, maintain determination when it gets tough, and build discipline into your life. *Then* confidence arrives.

It's okay to start small, like doing something for three days. Building trust, and therefore confidence, with yourself is a critical piece to your success with money. As an example, if you don't trust yourself, then you won't follow through on a commitment to save $500 a month. If you don't trust yourself, then you will likely overspend and not feel good about investing in your future.

I have worked with clients ranging from those who invest $100 a month into retirement accounts to those who invest millions of dollars with complex strategies. I see one common thread with all of them, and that is the ability to trust themselves with their decisions with money.

As a financial advisor and coach, I recognize that my clients had to trust themselves to reach out to me for support and guidance with their money and investments. They were able to trust me and my team because of our years of experience and knowledge. Even though I might be a sound voice of reason and insight, I always remind my clients to trust themselves. I am never there to override their insights and choices. I am simply there to guide, educate, and give expert direction. I want all of my clients to have strong self-trust because this leads to their ultimate success. And this is what I want you to experience.

It is extremely important for you to acknowledge and see the truth about your finances. If you don't trust yourself with how you manage your money, your money won't grow the way it could.

TRUST YOURSELF

Many people feel overwhelmed with the topic of managing money and investing money. This overwhelm is usually rooted in two areas. One, people aren't educated on how to manage or invest their money. Or two, they don't trust themselves with money and therefore are overwhelmed and want to avoid all topics regarding money.

This book tackles both. My desire is to clear out ALL of the overwhelm for you so that you feel a deep peace and confidence regarding your experience managing and growing your money. I will provide the tools and framework you need to be fully educated on the concepts that will help you create money success. It's okay to not know. Be kind with yourself, love yourself.

I want you to feel at ease and completely empowered in all aspects of understanding and growing your money. This is why *Money Loves You* is a whole NEW way to work with money. And that is why this method is going to work for you!

Remember, financial education and investing concepts are not taught to the masses. Sit in the place of not knowing and you will actually learn so much more easily.

As you become more educated and learn from your mistakes, you will establish greater trust with yourself. This increases your confidence in the financial decisions you make as you move forward in life.

But before you start to learn the tools and concepts that will guide you on your journey to truly feeling as though *money loves you*, we need to examine your own ability to trust yourself with money. I have a few questions for you to ask yourself.

Be honest with yourself as you answer these questions; all progress starts by telling the truth. Only *you* will see these answers. By doing this, you can build a new foundation of self-trust as you continue through this book with me.

1. Do you trust yourself with how you spend money?

    Yes   No

2. When you have extra money, are you aware of where the money goes?

    Yes   No

3. When you make a commitment to save a certain amount of money every month, do you follow through with that commitment?

    Yes   No

4. When you see an item for sale that you really want, do you:

    a. purchase it, *knowing* that you have the money to pay for it, or

    b. purchase it, *hoping* that there is money in the bank?

5. When you make an investment and the value goes down, what is your response?

    a. Immediately contact your advisor and tell them to sell it.

    b. Trust yourself, your trusted advisor, and the process.

    c. Beat yourself up, saying that you should never have invested in the first place.

This might make you feel ashamed or want to make yourself "wrong" for how you answered these questions. This is never my intention and those feelings won't help you with your money. Instead, they will actually stop the flow of money and keep you stuck. So, if those feelings crept up while you were answering, now is the time to take a deep breath and let them go. If you need help on this process, I will walk you through it in detail in Chapter 7.

This is a reminder that YOU have everything you need within you to create the aspirations and dreams you want for your life regarding money. And you have it all within you to commit and take the actions necessary to have these aspirations become real in your life.

I have seen clients from all over the country, in many different money situations, create success when they realized they had everything they needed within and truly learned how to trust themselves.

TRUST YOURSELF

Part of trusting yourself is investing in yourself. If you wanted to develop your speaking skills, you would hire a speaking coach. If you wanted to become an Ironman athlete, the quickest way to achieve this would be to hire an Ironman coach. If you want to fast track your wealth, hire a financial coach. All great athletes, actors, and businesses have taken the step of hiring a coach.

Trusting yourself to hire the right financial coach* will take you places you can't get to alone. It's hard to know what we don't know.

If you want support in finding a great financial coach, visit my company's website here:

Money Loves You Mindset Principle

You have everything you need within
and must truly trust yourself.

A common thread in millionaires I work with is their ability to trust themselves with their decisions about money.

MONEY LOVES YOU NOTE

CHAPTER SEVEN

TRANSFORM YOUR BELIEFS

Understanding the power of our words

Did you hear about the experiment IKEA did with two plants and the power of words? It is an excellent example of how negative and positive words impact results. If you don't know this story, it is an amazing example that will lend itself to your own experience with your thoughts and money.

The IKEA experiment involved two plants that were the exact same species. Both had the same environment, same soil, and were watered equally. There was only one differentiating factor: they were told different words. One plant was exposed to a recording of horrible words like, "You look rotten. You're not even green," while the other plant was exposed to a recording of positive words like, "Seeing you blossom makes me happy."

Each plant was exposed to these words for 30 days. At the end of the 30 days, the plant that was exposed to mean and negative statements was wilted and discolored, almost dead, while the plant that was spoken to with love was thriving and healthy (find study here: https://youtu.be/Yx6UgfQreYY).

If words are that impactful on a plant (that doesn't have a brilliant mind like ours), doesn't that make you wonder how your words and thoughts are impacting you and your money? What are you saying about your money and to your money? You probably don't know that answer right now since many thoughts about money go unnoticed, yet they are always running in the background. These thoughts and words are impacting your results with money.

I have found that tracking our thoughts is much more fruitful than tracking our money. Tracking our money, a.k.a. BUDGETING, is like treating the symptom instead of treating the root cause, which in this case is our mindset. When we get our mindset right, everything else falls into place.

I want to give you space to be empowered with your money by actually knowing what you think and say about and to your money. What you think about and say to your money is the mirror of what you think about and say to yourself. It's a great way to see the truth of your thoughts, feelings, and beliefs about yourself.

It's time to revisit the subconscious mind and start editing the stories and eliminating the limiting beliefs—what I call Wealth Busters—that hold us back. When we hold negative beliefs in connection to money, all we are doing is shutting money out and not allowing ourselves to receive it.

Transforming these limiting beliefs will open you up to take inspired action and pull you into your abundant future.

To do this you will need to learn and incorporate the following:

- an awareness to your Wealth Busters that sabotage your abundant future
- a willingness to accept that what got you here, *won't get you* to the *next level.*
- an understanding that not knowing what you don't know **is** limiting your abundance
- an understanding that transformation must occur for new results to show up.
- a willingness to **be** something different to get different results
- an understanding that your Wealth Busters are your greatest insight to the way forward

TRANSFORM YOUR BELIEFS

- using your Wealth Busters to teach you the path ahead
- **transforming your shame into your fame**

Wealth Buster Practice

This practice will support you in seeing the limiting thoughts and beliefs that hold you back from being your best and then help you bust through them! You might feel you want to breeze through this chapter without taking time to do the exercises, but I encourage you to dig into this work.

When I took the time to understand what my limiting beliefs were—*I'm not smart enough, I don't belong here, I'm not good enough*—and then completed the Wealth Buster exercise, I found my freedom and peace. Money became a by-product of getting out of my own way, I stopped my self-sabotage behaviors, and I allowed more abundance and miracles to come in.

Doing this self-discovery work is hard and uncomfortable, but it's so liberating and rewarding when you get to the root problems and transform them into powerful strongholds and positive beliefs. Often we are dealing with symptoms of a problem and aren't willing, or don't know how, to take the time to dig down and mine our subconscious minds. The subconscious mind holds so much power. Unsurprisingly, without our conscious direction and superconscious support, our subconscious can sabotage our efforts in life.

Wealth Buster Exercise

I love this saying from Blair Enns: "You cannot read the label from inside the jar."[6] It is hard to hear our own inner thoughts because we get so used to them. They become the white noise in the background of our lives. If you can see them, it can be easier to identify and expose them for the drain they are on your wealth and love for yourself.

Read through the Wealth Busters below and circle all those that you have thought or possibly said to yourself. If you have some that are not on this list, please write them in the space below.

Disclosures:

---

[6] Blair Enns, "Protecting Your Superpower," Win Without Pitching®, https://www.winwithoutpitching.com/superpower-protection/, acquired November 9, 2023.

Wealth Busters:

- I'll never have enough money.
- I'm not good with money.
- I don't know how to do it.
- No matter what I do, it's never enough.
- I'm afraid to spend my money.
- I don't want to look at my money.
- I don't want to pay my bills.
- I feel guilty for making more money.
- I am guilty for not making enough money.
- I make money but can't keep it.
- I fear success.
- More money, more problems.
- It's lonely at the top
- People will resent me if I succeed.
- I don't want to be found out.
- It's hard to keep money.
- No one's going to hire me.
- I'm not worthy of making money or keeping money.
- I won't be loved if I don't make money.
- I won't be accepted if I don't make money.
- I won't belong if I don't have money.
- I'll be alone.
- If I make money, I will finally be loved.
- I shouldn't be making money.
- I don't want the responsibility of more money.
- I don't want to stand out.
- I'm afraid to be seen as rich or wealthy.
- I am afraid of being judged.
- I'm embarrassed because I don't have enough money.
- I have nice things and I don't want to be judged.
- I judge myself.
- Money is too overwhelming.

TRANSFORM YOUR BELIEFS

- If I can't do it right, then I don't want to do it.
- I'm not smart enough.
- Money is bad. If I make money I will, by association, be bad.
- Money is corrupt. If I make money I will, by association, be corrupt.
- Money creates entitlement. If I make money I will, by association, be entitled.
- Money is overindulgence.
- I will run out of money.
- I fear that I will get taken advantage of.
- I will lose money if I invest in the stock market.
- Who do I think I am to make money?
- It's different for me; I can't make money.
- _____
- _____
- _____

How'd you do? Can you see what your recurring thoughts and patterns are? I am excited for you because this is the beginning of being able to recognize how you are holding yourself captive by them.

The exercises and questions throughout this book are designed to help you lovingly uncover the limiting beliefs that you hold about money and, subsequently, yourself.

It takes courage and work to open the subconscious mind and poke around for unpleasant beliefs and experiences that have happened in your life. Allowing yourself to go back and feel the emotions that you might have suppressed or avoided at the time—to survive—is a critical piece in your wealth journey. This process IS the stepping stone that leads you to creating the freedom you desire. It is through the dismantling of your Wealth Busters that you will become empowered with your money. I know this can be difficult and uncomfortable, but stay with it and be brave.

The next step is to look back over the statements you circled. Which one has the most umph, juice, or emotion behind it? Start with that one and follow the prompts below. I invite you to find a quiet place away from distractions and take your time going through these seven steps.

Once you are in a space that feels good to you, I want you to start by saying the following to yourself, either out loud or internally. Take a few moments to let each statement resonate in your mind before moving onto the next statement.

I am willing to change.
I am willing to change my story.
I am willing to look at my limiting beliefs.
I am willing to admit that I don't know what I don't know.
I am willing to be, do, and act in new and different ways.
I know that my limiting beliefs are some of my greatest teachers and by doing this exercise intently, with complete belief and trust in myself, I have the power to rid myself of these Wealth Busters forever.

Now take a few moments to let the above statements resonate together in your mind.

TRANSFORM YOUR BELIEFS

Step 1. Awareness

Close your eyes and focus your thoughts on your Wealth Buster statement. Allow yourself to see this as a limiting belief holding you back from what you desire. While you are focusing on this Wealth Buster statement, notice and become aware of any thoughts, feelings, and beliefs that arise. How does this belief make you feel? Do you know where it originated? Do you see an image? Did a painful memory surface? Write down in the space below any thoughts, feelings, memories, ideas, or images that presented themselves to you.

_____

_____

_____

_____

_____

_____

_____

_____

_____

_____

_____

_____

_____

_____

_____

_____

Step 2. Acceptance

Accept the Wealth Buster. Accept that this has been your limiting belief, BE in the emotions of it, and name the feelings. These could be fear, worry, guilt, anger, resentment, heartbrokenness, loneliness, embarrassment, humiliation, avoidance, disappointment, shame, or others. Close your eyes and be in those emotions as you think about this limiting belief and how it's held you back in life. You may want to stand up, or walk around, or beat a pillow, or cry, or yell and scream. While going for a run might help you physically, don't run away from your emotions internally. *Allow yourself to feel them.*

For many people, it is only natural to want to ignore or numb any feelings that don't feel comfortable. That's okay! Moving away from discomfort makes complete sense. And, if you really want freedom with your finances, then you must be able to BE with the uncomfortable feelings in a safe and loving way, as you are doing right now. The stories and emotions that show up around money are most likely negative feelings that are usually linked back to either how you were raised or challenging experiences you have had with money.

Write down the emotions you just experienced. If there are any actions you want to associate with these emotions, feel free to add those.

For example: when I accepted my anger I wanted to . . .

_____

_____

_____

_____

_____

_____

_____

_____

TRANSFORM YOUR BELIEFS

Step 3. Recall

Using the emotion(s) from the above writing and the Wealth Buster you identified, ask yourself where this limiting belief came from. I want you to recall a time in which you experienced this emotion and limiting belief. Was it recent or a distant memory? Have you labeled this emotion or limiting belief? Is this a new experience or an old pattern?

If you are unable to recall a situation, ask yourself, *what is my earliest memory around money?* In the space below, write your memory or any other situations that present themselves.

How old were you? What was the situation? Who else was there? Set the entire scene. Do you remember what you were wearing? What time of day was it? Write in as much detail as you can, even if it feels trivial or insignificant. Now, acting from your superconscious, pretend you have never heard this story before. It is brand new information. Re-read your story and act as if this is the first time you are hearing this story.

_____

_____

_____

_____

_____

_____

_____

_____

_____

_____

_____

_____

Step 4. Reveal

What did you learn about your story? Was it tied to a limiting belief or Wealth Buster? What was revealed to you as you were hearing this story for the first time? Did you see your story in a new way? Did you find compassion or empathy for yourself or someone else? Were there surprises? On the lines below, record what has been revealed to you.

_____

_____

_____

_____

_____

_____

_____

_____

_____

_____

_____

_____

_____

_____

_____

_____

_____

_____

_____

Step 5. Reimagine

Now it's time to have a little fun and use your imagination. You are in complete control of this memory. Imagine you are the director of this memory. Allow yourself to go back and re-create it the way you would have wanted it to play out. What would you want to change about the experience? What would you want to say that wasn't spoken? How would you express your feelings? Would you react in a different way? How would you reimagine the memory? Allow other people who were involved to say what wasn't spoken—something you really needed to hear. Completely re-create the interaction. Write down what is helpful as you re-create and reframe this old memory with words, actions, and feelings.

Taking time in this step leads to busting through this Wealth Buster. When you re-create the experience or memory that came up for you and REIMAGINE it, you get to rewrite your story.

Step 6. Receive

Find the lessons and gifts of this experience or memory and how those lessons or gifts relate to who you are today. How did those lessons or gifts shape your current self? Can you see any positives that came from this experience? What did this teach you about yourself? Is there a different perspective you can see now that you have reimagined this experience?

I know it may seem difficult to find the gift in an unpleasant memory or a negative experience, but if you can find one—and I promise you, you can—you will be able to release it and break free from what holds you back.

I invite you to take a moment and see what it is that you received or learned from that past experience. Ask yourself the question, close your eyes, and be still. Emotions might surface. It's okay to be with the discomfort of painful emotions in a safe and loving way. Breathe and find stillness. In the stillness, a message will often be given to you. If not? No worries, trust that you will discover the answer when the time is right. On the lines below, write your lesson or gift.

_____

_____

_____

_____

_____

_____

_____

_____

_____

_____

_____

Step 7. Release

As you think about this experience and view it through a new lens and see how it shaped who you are today, can you feel gratitude? Is there a possibility for peace, forgiveness, love for this memory, experience, or another person that was involved? You may not like what has happened in your past, but the lessons and gifts you've discovered can serve your future.

Experiencing gratitude is one of the fastest ways to release yourself from old patterns of emotions and current problems. Gratitude has the power to transform your thoughts and beliefs in an instant. Allow this.

Spend a moment feeling gratitude, forgiveness, and love for the past situation or experience. And don't forget about feeling gratitude, forgiveness, and love for yourself!

Often the person we need to forgive most is ourselves. See that younger version of you, extend grace and unconditional love, and let go of the past. Forgiveness is the way.

Forgiveness is an intentional decision to let go of the emotions that come from a painful experience; this could be anger or resentment. The experience or situation that hurt or offended you might always be with you, but when you can forgive, it no longer holds you captive. The grip on you is released; you are free. When you can feel true forgiveness, you will create more space for love in your life. Love is the door to new beginnings and new opportunities in your life.

Write down what you are grateful for.

_____

_____

_____

_____

_____

_____

_____

This is deep and challenging work but it's also the key to unlocking abundance for your future. *If this brings up a very painful memory, I highly recommend working through this with a professional therapist.*

When you can get to the root of your beliefs and transform them, watch out—the sky's the limit! By doing this work, I have seen massive shifts in my own journey, and I know you will see those shifts in your journey too.

I encourage you to revisit this process for each of the Wealth Busters you circled at the beginning of this chapter and anytime in the future you are feeling stuck or notice a recurring thought or belief that isn't serving you.

Let's look at Amanda's journey in busting through her limiting belief.

TRANSFORM YOUR BELIEFS

Amanda's Journey

Let's follow the story of Amanda. She is in her late forties and feels the urgency to get serious about saving and investing her money but just constantly feels stuck when making decisions to grow her wealth. She knows something is holding her back so she has decided to embark on a transformative journey to discover and break free from her scarcity-mindset limiting belief.

Step 1. Awareness

Amanda has always struggled with a scarcity mindset. She has constantly worried about not having enough money, opportunities, or resources. She has created a good life for herself but one that doesn't bring her the joy, freedom, or passion she desires. She has a career as a pharmaceutical sales representative and has been able to pay her bills, but it's never enough. Her savings is small and while she hasn't really looked into it, she knows it's not enough to take care of her in retirement.

She took a couple of weekend trips with her girlfriends last year, but those weren't the tropical getaway she has been dreaming of. She recently received a bonus from her company and was so excited to purchase a designer purse. Finally! She feels like she has some money to get something she really wants, something luxurious, purely fun, and frivolous. She is so excited on the drive to the store and is constantly thinking about spending this money. As she pulls into the parking lot, she gets a call from her contractor. She is getting new floors put in at home and they discovered areas of dry rot. It is going to cost $5,000 more than she expected. Amanda hangs up the phone and starts sobbing. "I will never have enough money. EVER!" This thought keeps circling in her head. She cries into the steering wheel and knows that she needs to spend this bonus on her home instead of what she really wants—the new designer handbag. She hears the thought again and again,

I will never have enough money. She thinks back to all the times she struggled with money: her divorce, college, pulling double shifts at the local diner. Deep down, Amanda knows she can figure this out. The belief, *I will never have enough money*, is not one she wants to use to write the story of her life. These painful memories and feelings give Amanda a new awareness of the thoughts ruling her mind. On the drive home, she decides it's time to confront her beliefs, fears, and limitations so she can create a path to change.

Step 2. Acceptance

When Amanda gets home, she looks around her place and notices all the things money has bought. She knows she can figure this out. She doesn't have to live and feel like this. Amanda goes to her favorite chair and sits quietly. She allows herself to see and become aware of her thoughts. She begins to explore the emotions she felt in the car and begins naming them: fear, anxiety, desperation, and insecurity. She knows fear is the strongest emotion she is experiencing. Gently, she accepts that she is fearful and decides not to run away from it. She befriends this emotion. She feels it in her chest, her jaw, and her hands. She breathes slowly and deeply. Even though she really wants to move away from these sensations and realizations, she allows herself to feel and deliberately focuses on the fear. After a few minutes of deep breathing, she feels a change in her emotion. The fear, while still present, is not gripping her mind and body. She can look at it for what it is: an emotion.

Step 3. Recall

With her eyes closed, Amanda remembers a specific experience from her childhood and realizes that her scarcity mindset is deeply rooted in her fear of never having enough. When Amanda was 15, her family faced financial difficulties when her dad lost his job. She didn't understand what that meant, her father losing his job. Couldn't he just get another one?

Amanda remembers one particular day sitting on her bed doing her biology homework when all of a sudden, the door to her parents' bedroom slammed shut and she heard the muffled sounds of her parents arguing. She remembered feeling scared. Raised voices were not the norm in her home. She got off her bed, went to her door, opened it slowly, and walked toward her parents' room to investigate. She didn't have to walk far before she could clearly hear her parents screaming at each other about money. They were calling each other names Amanda had never heard them use before and she became so scared she ran back into her room, turned her radio up as loud as it could go, and grabbed her biology textbook to distract herself from her parents' yelling.

Shortly after this incident, Amanda's dad moved out and her mom told Amanda that they were getting a divorce. Amanda was going to have to make changes. The biggest change was that Amanda had to quit the gymnastics team. Her family could no longer afford the cost. This memory

TRANSFORM YOUR BELIEFS

left a lasting impression on her and scripted a limiting belief of *I will never have enough money* deep into her subconscious.

Amanda takes a deep breath and walks through the memory again, this time with her superconscious in charge, imagining she had never experienced this story. Though still upsetting and painful, Amanda is able to see the memory from a completely new vantage point, one that births compassion for herself, her family, and the life she has lived.

Step 4. Reveal

Still sitting in her favorite chair and new to this memory, she is able to see the terror and dread she experienced as her parents were yelling at each other. She feels deep compassion for that scared, uncertain young teenager. She takes careful notice of the biology textbook and remembers her teacher Ms. Foyle, who had encouraged Amanda in her biology class. Ms. Foyle was especially warm and helpful in the months after Amanda's parents divorced.

Amanda becomes overwhelmed with gratitude for the kindness and tenderness Ms. Foyle showed when Amanda was in deep need of extra care. She smiles as she thinks about the song she blasted—"Time After Time"—and remembers how much she loved Cyndi Lauper, and how she and her best girlfriends used to sing the chorus at the top of their lungs and then fall into laughter at how badly they sang. She had forgotten all those good memories because the fear and terror had so overwhelmed her.

Step 5. Reimagine

Filled with compassion and gratitude, and some nostalgia for Cyndi Lauper, Amanda decides to reimagine this story. She thinks of her favorite movie and pretends that she is to direct this scene. However, she fires the original script writer and takes it upon herself to rewrite it. She uses her imagination and this time, she envisions her younger self going to her parents' door. She knocks hard and confidently on the door; the screaming stops. She expresses her fear and worry at her parents' behavior. Her parents are embarrassed and somewhat ashamed that they let their emotions rage out of control and scare their child. They give her what she needs: an apology and comfort. They assure her that their impending divorce is not her fault.

The three of them sit in Amanda's room and talk openly and kindly about the struggles they've been experiencing. Amanda can see their deep love for each other and also the need for separation. In her mind, she begins to feel compassion for her parents and understands how exhausting and painful their divorce would be for them. She begins to feel compassion for herself and remembers how difficult that time was for her: her dad moving out, changing her whole world and routines, not being able to participate in gymnastics, and carrying the daily fears of *what will happen to me next? Will mom lose her job? Will we have to leave our house?*

Step 6. Receive

Amanda notices her pain transforming as she reimagines her past. In imagining holding her parents accountable for their behavior, she is able to accept their regret and apology. She experiences a wave of compassion cultivated from reimaging what she needed at that time. Without this difficult time, she could have never grasped the importance of her resilience, grit, and perseverance. Of course, she wishes she didn't have to experience the pain and fear that ultimately led to long-lasting feelings of anxiety and insecurity, but through the challenges she finds her scarcity mindset had, in fact, made her appreciate the value of what truly matters in life—and to her, that is love and resilience.

Step 7. Release

Amanda feels a deep sense of peace for the past experience that led her on this journey of self-discovery. She releases her Wealth Buster—*I will never have enough money*—and forgives her parents for their financial struggles and separation, knowing they had done their best. She also forgives herself for carrying this scarcity mindset for so long.

With her heart filled with gratitude, forgiveness, and unconditional love for herself, her parents, and her past, Amanda feels a profound sense of peace. She feels the grip of her old scarcity beliefs loosening, and she knows she is on the path to embracing abundance in all aspects of her life.

Feeling empowered in a way she hasn't felt in quite some time, Amanda decides to mark the occasion of this transformation. She grabs her phone, puts in her earphones, and blasts "Time after Time," which had been playing in her memory. She moves and dances and scream-sings the chorus. She knows any time this Wealth Buster surfaces, she can put this song on and return to the new thoughts and beliefs she created.

TRANSFORM YOUR BELIEFS

Amanda's journey of reprogramming her subconscious mind not only transforms her relationship with money but also with her parents as the forgiveness she feels in her heart brings the walls down. This shift allows her to live a more fulfilled and abundant life. She realizes that by embracing her past and the lessons it has taught her, she can step into a brighter future, free from the scarcity mindset that once held her back.

The Wealth Belief Process

Now that you have started to see what thoughts have been running your system, I will help you create a new set of thoughts to use in connection with money. You've learned how to let go of the limiting beliefs. Now you can cultivate and embody the new mindset, leaning on help from the superconscious, and embodying the Money Loves You mindset: The Wealth Beliefs.

Beliefs come from thoughts. I want to introduce new thoughts into your relationship with money. Over time, new thoughts bring new feelings and behaviors, which then transform into new beliefs that will ultimately become your Wealth Beliefs.

Below are a few examples of potential new thoughts in connection to money. Go through the list below, as you did with the Wealth Busters, and circle any that resonate with you. Or, use the space below to write your own. If you are having trouble finding one that resonates with you, I suggest starting with "Money Loves Me." After reading this far in the book, there is a part of you, however small, that truly believes *Money Loves You.*

Wealth Beliefs:

- Money loves me.
- I have all the money I need.
- I am open to receiving money.
- I am generous with money.
- I am empowered with money.
- I am smart enough to do this.
- I am enough.
- I have clarity with my money.
- I have everything I need.
- I am on my path to financial independence.
- I am financially free.
- I have financial stability.
- I treat money with respect.
- I am a good investor.
- I make smart decisions with my money.
- I am abundant.
- I can take risks.
- I feel secure.
- I can trust myself with money.
- I can trust myself.
- I am capable of having a healthy relationship with money and my partner.
- I am capable of making the necessary changes to build financial security.

Step 1. Willingness

Take the most prominent Wealth Belief that you circled above. Like in the Wealth Buster process, I want you to find a quiet place to sit calmly and focus on this belief. Have willingness to be open, have faith, and believe that abundance is ahead.

TRANSFORM YOUR BELIEFS

Step 2. Consciousness

As you sit with this belief, are there any emotions coming up? Any thoughts that aren't in alignment with where you want to be? It's okay if there are. Let them arise, extend grace to yourself, and bring your thoughts back to your Wealth Belief. Let go of the limiting mindset and come back to your superconscious self.

Step 3. Momentum

Everytime you release a limiting belief, focus on and attune your mind to the mindset you want to embody; you are creating momentum. And, when you create momentum, you are taking action and eliciting change. The consistency of returning to the mindset you want to embody is the active change you will need. Reflect on the quote from earlier in the chapter: "What got you here won't get you there."

Your thoughts are the driving force to your relationship and ultimately, your results with money. It all starts in the mind. When we can begin to master our thoughts, we will feel differently, and this will drive new behaviors. You've got this.

Money Loves You Mindset Principle

Tracking our thoughts is much more fruitful than tracking our money.

Often the person we need to forgive most is ourselves. See that younger version of you, extend grace and unconditional love, and let go of the past. Forgiveness is the way.

MONEY LOVES YOU NOTE

CHAPTER EIGHT

REVEAL YOUR MONEY IDENTITY

Our identities are simply what we see ourselves as—the core parts of who we are—based upon our thoughts, feelings, beliefs, actions, and experiences. Our identity is shaped within us and it's what we believe to be true about ourselves. Our identities are an invisible power in our lives that will either hold us back or advance our pursuits to achieve our dreams.

The beautiful thing about identity is it's not fixed and it evolves over time. It can be influenced by personal growth, changing circumstances, new experiences, and shifts in our beliefs and values. You know where I am going. . . . YES, I want you to upgrade your identity with money to serve you better.

Let me give you a simple example of an identity. When I started dating my husband, Chris, I worked at Blockbuster Video. I wore the logo'd blue polo shirt with khakis and helped customers find and rent their desired VHS tapes (I am so thankful we don't have to worry about rewinding videos anymore!). I worked the evening shift so I would get home at 1:30 a.m. and sleep in until 11:00 a.m. Chris went to work at 6:30 a.m. and went to bed at 9:00 p.m. We lived in different states so, using my flip phone, I would call him from my Honda Prelude during my drive home. He wouldn't even remember our conversations the next day because he'd been talking to me in his sleep.

I clearly identified as a night owl and he identified as a morning person. Our life experiences created our behaviors and our identities were formed. After I moved to the Oregon Coast, I found myself keeping the same schedule because after all, I was a night owl. This was my thought and true belief about myself.

I found a job as a waitress at a cafe and the shift started at 6:00 a.m. I remember almost not taking the job because I wondered how the heck I would ever get myself out of bed at 5:00 in the morning. My thoughts went crazy. *Can I really do this? How am I going to be able to function at six in the morning? That is like the middle of the night!* The need to pay for my apartment and expenses was greater than my fear of getting up early, so I took the job.

Taking inspiration from Chris, I set my thoughts on being positive and telling myself, *I can do this*. I started getting up early and making it to work on time; after several weeks, I actually enjoyed being up that early. In fact, when I got off work at 2:00 in the afternoon, I felt like I had my whole day in front of me.

My thoughts led to different behaviors, then my behaviors changed my identity, and now I am a morning person. To this day it is how I identify and I enjoy waking up early.

We often don't fully appreciate the immense power of our thoughts and their positive or negative influence on us. Our thoughts turn into feelings and our feelings make us act in certain ways. Over time, our actions and behaviors become our identity. When we are aware of our identity and what we want in life, we can then unpack the results and make different choices to support our desired vision.

One of the keys to my success has been to understand and find ways to constantly upgrade my own identity. This has happened through working on my mindset and personal growth by reading books, stepping outside my comfort zone, and investing in coaching programs that hold me to a higher standard. These books and programs constantly inspire me to think differently and take on new perspectives.

Now it's your turn. Can you pick out an identity you believe about yourself? This could be about anything, like your health or career, and also your

REVEAL YOUR MONEY IDENTITY

money. For example, if you work out and train consistently, you might see yourself as fit or as an athlete. If you are a doctor or the CEO of a company, your career will naturally be part of your identity.

What is your current view of your money identity? It could be hard to answer this question. That is why I created a quiz to help you reveal your money identity. Scan the QR code to take the quiz.

In working with clients from all walks of life, I have discovered that there are a handful of money identities.

Each money identity has specific strengths and weaknesses based on their financial behaviors and attitudes. Let's take a look at them.

Financial Avoiders:

Financial avoiders have an overall sense of hopelessness and avoidance with money. They often feel fear, anxiety, and helplessness when thinking about money and don't feel confident in their ability to manage money. Rooted in a past of shame, either from their caretakers or their own money mistakes, they have a gloomy outlook for the future. This makes them want to not plan at all and just live for today (or yesterday). A feeling of overwhelm is often present.

Strengths of financial avoiders can include the following:

- **Being present-focused**: Financial avoiders often live in the moment. This can make them good at enjoying the present without worrying excessively about the future.
- **Resourcefulness**: In some cases, their avoidance of financial matters may lead them to be resourceful in finding ways to get by with limited resources.
- **Resilience**: Financial challenges can often build resilience. Over time, they may become better at coping with adversity, managing stress, and finding ways to navigate difficult financial situations.

This resilience can be a valuable trait that extends beyond financial matters, helping them overcome various life challenges.

Weaknesses of the financial avoiders can include the following:

- **Financial instability**: The avoidance of financial planning and management can lead to financial instability. Without proper planning, they may struggle to meet financial goals and emergencies.
- **Ineffective money management**: Avoiding money-related issues often results in poor money management. This can lead to unnecessary levels of debt, missed financial opportunities, and a lower quality of life.
- **Dependency**: In extreme cases, some financial avoiders may become financially dependent on others, such as family members or partners, which can strain relationships and limit their independence.

It's important to note that while these strengths and weaknesses are associated with the financial avoider money identity, individuals can change their attitudes and behaviors toward money with the right support, education, and mindset shift. Seeking professional financial counselors or therapy may be beneficial for those who identify with this money identity to help them address their avoidance issues and develop healthier financial habits.

Novice Money-seekers:

Novice money-seekers have never been educated about money and often feel stuck because they simply don't know where to start. They desire to be smart with money but don't know where to begin or what to do. They would do the right thing if they had the guidance to make wise decisions with money.

They often make a lot of money but they aren't great at saving it, simply because they don't know where to start. They spend easily on things that matter to them.

Strengths of novice money-seekers can include the following:

- **Desire to learn**: Novice money-seekers have a genuine desire and curiosity to become financially literate and make wise decisions with their money. This eagerness to learn and improve their financial situation is a significant strength.
- **Income potential**: Novice money-seekers have great income potential due to their desire to learn and grow. This can be a valuable asset if they acquire the financial knowledge and skills to manage their money effectively.
- **Spending on values**: They are selective about where they spend their money, focusing on things that matter to them. This means they may prioritize spending on experiences or items that align with their values and goals more easily.

Weaknesses of the novice money-seekers can include the following:

- **Lack of financial education**: The primary weakness of novice money-seekers is their lack of financial education. Without proper guidance, they may struggle to understand fundamental financial concepts, which may lead to poor decision-making.
- **Limited savings**: Despite earning well, their lack of financial knowledge and guidance may result in inadequate savings or investments. This can leave them vulnerable to financial emergencies and hinder their ability to achieve long-term goals.
- **Dependency on external guidance**: The dependence on external sources for financial decisions can be a weakness since it may make them vulnerable to poor advice or decisions in the absence of professional guidance.

It's important for novice money-seekers to take proactive steps to educate themselves about finances and seek out reliable financial resources. They should consider working with an expert—either a licensed financial advisor or coach—to develop a solid financial plan. With the right support and education, they can transform their eagerness to learn into effective money-management skills and achieve their financial goals.

Financial Free-spirits:

Financial free-spirits love life and live for today. They are often indifferent to money and really see it as a necessary evil. They go back and forth from wanting to have financial freedom and preparing for the future to getting sidetracked and wanting what brings them joy today. This often leads to overspending on all types of experiences and things that are often impulse buys. Retail therapy is alive and well with these free spirits.

Strengths of the financial free-spirits can include the following:

- **Enjoyment of life**: Financial free-spirits have a strong emphasis on living in the moment and enjoying life. This quality can lead to a fulfilling and enjoyable lifestyle because they prioritize experiences and happiness.
- **Flexibility and adaptability**: They are adaptable and open to new experiences. Their willingness to go with the flow can make them more resilient in the face of unexpected financial challenges or changes in circumstances.
- **Spontaneity**: Financial free-spirits embrace spontaneity, which can lead to exciting and memorable experiences. They are not bound by rigid financial plans and can take advantage of opportunities that arise.

Weaknesses of the financial free-spirits can include the following:

Limited financial security: Due to their tendency to prioritize immediate pleasures and impulse purchases, which translates to increased debt, financial free-spirits may lack the financial security needed to weather unexpected life events, such as medical emergencies, job loss, or economic downturns. This lack of financial security can leave them vulnerable to financial stress and hardship when faced with such challenges, potentially impacting their overall well-being.

Lack of financial planning: They often struggle with long-term financial planning. Their focus on immediate gratification may prevent them from adequately saving for important life events like retirement or emergencies.

Potential for regret: Over time, financial free-spirits may experience regret for not having saved or invested wisely for the future. This can lead to anxiety or stress when they realize they are unprepared for financial challenges or major life transitions.

It's essential for financial free-spirits to strike a balance between enjoying the present and planning for the future. They epitomize the earlier concept of holding two opposing truths. While embracing spontaneity and enjoying life is important, they can benefit from setting some financial boundaries and goals to ensure financial stability and security in the long run. Developing money management skills and seeking financial advice can help them make more-informed financial decisions while still savoring the joys of today.

Savvy Stewards:

Savvy stewards love to save money, have smart or low debt, and give themselves goals to accomplish. They tend to be responsible and conservative in their risk level and value security. To organize their money life, they will often have "buckets" for money with different names for each bucket. And they find it hard to live life for today or make big purchases because they don't want to see their money disappear.

Strengths of the savvy stewards can include the following:

Strong savings habits: Savvy stewards excel at saving money and are diligent in building a financial cushion. Their disciplined approach to saving can lead to financial security and the ability to weather unexpected expenses.

Low debt: They tend to have low levels of debt, which can contribute to their overall financial stability. By avoiding excessive debt, they reduce the financial stress associated with high-interest payments.

Being goal-oriented: Savvy stewards set and work toward financial goals. Their goal-oriented nature helps them achieve long-term financial objectives, such as saving for retirement or major purchases.

Weaknesses of the savvy stewards can include the following:

Difficulty enjoying the present: One of the primary weaknesses of savvy stewards is their reluctance to spend money on immediate pleasures or experiences. Their focus on saving and security can make it challenging for them to enjoy the present and indulge in life's pleasures.

Risk aversion: They tend to be risk-averse and may miss out on potential investment opportunities or financial growth because they prioritize safety over potential returns. This can limit their wealth-building potential in the long run.

Overemphasis on money management: Their meticulous approach to managing and organizing their finances can sometimes lead to an obsession with money management. This obsession can cause stress and detract from other aspects of their life, including relationships and personal well-being.

While savvy stewards excel in financial responsibility, it's crucial for them to find a harmony between securing their future and savoring the present. Finding ways to allocate a portion of their finances for experiences and enjoyment can help them lead a more joyful and fulfilling life. Additionally, seeking guidance from financial advisors can help them optimize their investment strategies without compromising their risk tolerance.

Inspired Money-makers:

"I've got this and money loves me." Inspired money-makers understand money and it flows naturally for them. They are often a magnet for money, which creates confidence (sometimes too much), and they could potentially be at risk for being taken advantage of or investing speculatively. They enjoy investing and seeing their money grow. They are generous givers and feel abundant.

Strengths of the inspired money-makers can include the following:

Financial confidence: Inspired money-makers have a strong sense of confidence when it comes to money. They believe that money flows naturally to them and feel in control of their financial situation.

Financial magnetism: They often attract financial opportunities and have a knack for making money. This ability to attract wealth can lead to financial security and prosperity.

Being enthusiastic investors: Inspired money-makers enjoy investing and watching their money grow. Their enthusiasm for investing can lead to sound financial decisions and potentially lucrative returns.

Weaknesses of the inspired money-makers can include the following:

Overconfidence: Sometimes, their strong belief in their financial abilities can lead to overconfidence. This overconfidence may make them more susceptible to taking excessive risks or making speculative investments.

Potential for exploitation: Their confidence and willingness to invest can make them vulnerable to individuals or schemes that take advantage of their financial trust and optimism.

Generosity without boundaries: While being generous is a positive trait, inspired money-makers may give too freely and without boundaries, which can impact their own financial security and long-term goals.

It's essential for inspired money-makers to maintain a healthy integration of confidence and caution. While their financial magnetism and enthusiasm for investing are strengths, they should be vigilant about avoiding overly speculative investments and setting clear financial boundaries to protect their own financial interests. Seeking guidance from financial advisors can help them make informed decisions and ensure their generosity aligns with their long-term financial goals.

After reading about all the identities, which one or ones (you can have a combination) do you resonate with? Circle below:

- **Financial Avoider**
- **Novice Money-seeker**
- **Financial Free-spirit**
- **Savvy Steward**
- **Inspired Money-maker**

Celebrate your instinctual money identity. You have been wired to be a certain way with money; embrace and have fun with this. You also have a unique set of experiences that have impacted your thoughts, beliefs, and identity around money. You don't necessarily *need* to aspire to become a different identity type, because each has its own strengths and weaknesses, but you can if you want! It could be as simple as recognizing your positive attributes and allowing the strengths to pull you into the future as you stay aware of potential pitfalls.

No matter where your money identity lies right now, here is the great news: If you want to change your money identity, all you need to do is change your behavior and that starts with your thoughts. You get to choose the identity you want based on the behaviors you display. My hope is that this book is inspiring you to do just that. You tell yourself what you want to believe. You have the power to change.

I know what you are thinking: easier said than done. It can be hard looking at behaviors you are not proud of and it can stir or trigger emotions of fear, blame, and regret. This is normal and I encourage you to let these feelings go.

Let me remind you that you are fully empowered to change your money identity simply by seeing it and becoming aware of the behaviors that are holding you captive to that identity.

Let this be easy.

You don't have to worry about knowing how to change these behaviors *right now*. More on that later, as I will continue to guide you through a new way. I want you to understand that most behaviors around money are taught to us from a young age. That also means the behavior is a default—most humans don't know how to be ANY different.

Our identities hold potential that either keeps us in the status quo or is a power assist in pursuing our dreams. Realizing your potential is the ultimate self-care routine and a beautiful way of expressing love to yourself.

Money Loves You Mindset Principle

If you want to change your money identity, all you need to do is change your behavior and that starts with your thoughts. You get to choose the identity you want based on the behaviors you display. You have the power to change.

Identities are not fixed; they are fluid. Identity follows your behaviors.

Money Loves You Note

CHAPTER NINE

CREATE YOUR FREEDOM NOW

We can get so caught up in wanting to have it all that we get addicted to *doing* it all so then we can finally BE. Be happy. Be joyful. Be fulfilled. Be retired. Be a world traveler. Be a philanthropist. Be an artist. Be a reader. Be an entrepreneur.

The chase for HAVING that results in DOING can create overwhelm in our lives and our relationship to money. Oftentimes, we think that if we DO a lot, we will make a lot of money so we can HAVE a lot and THEN—only then—will we find the happiness that we are seeking.

But, if you were to interview a handful of millionaires you would find that they did not find happiness while they were chasing, hustling, and achieving their goals. They may have been *addicted* to the DOING that led to the money, but *happiness* wasn't waiting for them. In a lot of cases, the chase left them feeling empty and important relationships had been shattered.

If this process of having and doing doesn't result in happiness and freedom, which most of us are searching for, then we have to do things differently.

So, what if we flipped this concept?

It's the shift from:

HAVE. DO. BE.

to

BE. DO. HAVE.

What does this even mean? Let me explain . . .

This concept was originally taught by Stephen R. Covey in *The 7 Habits of Highly Effective People*. The **BE. DO. HAVE.** concept allows you to live in that future place **now**. Be your future self and *make decisions from that place*.

I've seen this multiple times: people will inherit wealth, just to spend it all within a short time frame. Why is this? They are unable to keep the money because they didn't become who they needed to be to keep that wealth. They did not have the skill set of trusting and loving themselves as the money came to them. They didn't connect to their future self while making money decisions, nor did they feel worthy of the wealth. People often feel they don't deserve the money, so they subconsciously do things to get rid of the money. The responsibility of money scared them and as a result it slipped right through their fingertips, leaving them filled with regret and despair.

Do you know how many of those people thought that their problems would finally be over now that they had a bank account full of money?

And did money solve their problems? Did they find the freedom and joy that they had been searching for? Maybe for a short, fleeting moment they felt free and happy. But it wasn't long-lasting. And that is because the *having* isn't what creates the result you are looking for.

I know this might be shocking, simply because most of us have been taught to believe that once we get the house of our dreams, that sports car in our garage, or that luxury vacation . . . we will finally feel content. But, I want you to think back to moments in your life when you did get that item. Maybe it was the first time, or fifth time, you purchased a new car. Those first few weeks you proudly drove your car with happiness bursting out of you. But within a few months, the newness wore off, the new car smell faded, the feelings of euphoria waned to routine, and the shine of happiness you so desired had dulled. You were once again on the hunt for fulfillment and freedom. We do this with relationships, money, business, and obtaining *things*. The truth is, these things are not what bring you the desired fulfillment and freedom that you are searching for.

In this next section, we will explore ways that will allow you to arrive at those desired feelings before you have all of the things you think you desire.

Example of HAVE. DO. BE.

Todd was a great pediatrician in his town. He had graduated top of his class from Baylor University and loved his job. He made around $400,000 a year, which allowed for a comfortable life with his wife, Emily, and their two kids. But Todd was very caught up in the **HAVE. DO. BE.** cycle. He had been taught this by his father who was always aiming to have more with the hope that with the more, they would finally be happy. It didn't work out for his dad, but that didn't stop the cycle with Todd. The cycle had found its way into Todd's life and he was running a million miles an hour to try to crack the code on life.

Todd worked 50 hours a week at his clinic and then pulled overtime on the weekends to make more money. He was determined to buy the house of his dreams so that they could finally be happy.

Along the way toward this big dream, he missed many of his son's baseball games and most evening dinners with his family. His wife would take the kids to playgrounds and the amusement park down the road on the weekends while he pulled the extra shifts. They had both agreed that the sacrifice of him being gone all the time was worth it so they could finally buy the house they had been dreaming of for years.

The day came when all of their hard work and sacrifice paid off. They proudly held the keys to their new home and felt the relief that only comes when you feel like you have made it. The problem is, that relief only lasted a little while because they soon learned that the dream house didn't make them happy like they'd expected it to. Instead, they still felt anxious and began searching for whatever held the new hope for happiness.

Maybe it was a vacation? Yes, surely that would finally make them fulfilled. Of course, with all of Todd's extra work hours and Emily raising the kids alone—obviously they needed a vacation.

But once again, after they obtained their dream trip to Disney World with their kids, they were left wanting more.

This cycle is a beast that is always hungry and no matter your attempts, strategies, or angles, the animal will never be full.

The **HAVE. DO. BE.** is the cycle most humans live in. It's the American dream. We place our focus first on HAVING all the things—the home, the car, the dream vacation, whatever it is for you—and this drives our behavior of DOING the activity we think we need to do to achieve the dream, and *then* we will arrive. Then we will be content. This is a recipe for hustle and burnout. It may work for the short term but not over the long term.

I invite you to take a minute and journal about if, and when, you have ever been stuck in the **HAVE. DO. BE.** cycle.

Ask yourself these questions.

1. Was there a time when I thought getting something tangible would make me happy?

2. If yes, what was it?

3. Did it make me happy in the short term or over the long term?

4. Has chasing the "wants" left me happier or hungrier?

5. Have I felt burned out in the process of obtaining the things?

BE. DO. HAVE.

Flipping this concept is the secret. It starts with understanding who you want to be in the future and then asking, "Why can't I be that person now?" Can you become a match for your future *self now*? Can you put yourself in that future place and make decisions from there, *now*?

Allowing yourself to BE is uncomfortable because often, you find your sense of self-worth in the doing, in the action, in the giving. It's like you are trying to win the prize or prove yourself worthy to yourself, your partner, others, or the world.

Our self-worth must be bigger than our net worth. Our concept of our internal value impacts our money! Our worth is innate. It is ours at birth. We have nothing to do, nothing to prove, nothing to defend; we have only to receive it, accept it, and step into the grace of what it does on our behalf. We must surrender the hustle and control to grasp this concept.

We can't earn or do our way into our worthiness; it is ours to embrace and embracing our worthiness is an act of self-love.

Our *feeling* of worthiness evolves over time with our experiences and learnings and as we grow and feel the shifts within. This expands our *awareness* of our self-worth—but our self-worth was there all along.

Our *sense* of worth expands with our ability to listen and receive, with our awareness shifting from the need to prove ourselves by doing and having to simply being. With this shift, it no longer matters what we have and do in the world but who we are and what we are becoming.

BE in your worth, BE more in your God-given abilities and talents, and listen to your still small voice that nudges you this way or that way. The more we play to our strengths and rely on our natural abilities, the more we see the blessings and abundance show up, not because we are now worthy but because we are living with purpose in pursuit of our desires.

Example of BE. DO. HAVE.

Sean was naturally pulled to wanting things—nice things. He desired a large house on the edge of the river, with windows in the house that he could sit by while he read and watched the river flow. He wanted a reliable SUV that he could take trips in with his wife, Becca, and their three kids. Sean loved the idea of nice dinners out with Becca and really wanted to surprise her with gifts. He was guilty of pursuing these dreams and caught in the **HAVE. DO. BE.** cycle, which only led to a deep level of burnout, exhaustion, and ultimately a job loss.

After he lost his job, he felt horrible. Fear and embarrassment began to drown him and because of this, he wasn't able to get a new job. After he learned about the **BE. DO. HAVE.** mindset shift, he restructured his life and thoughts. He began to focus on how he felt, right here, right now, in this present moment. He started to focus on feeling what he *wanted* to feel, even in his hardest moments. Even though his life wasn't going how he wanted, he chose to find joy in spite of his circumstances.

Sean would wake up early to spend time with his kids before they went to school. He found joy in their little voices and in making breakfast for his wife. He focused on feeling the relief he would feel when he once again had a job. But he didn't want just any job. He wanted his dream job. So, he began to feel as though he already had that dream job—the one where he worked from his home office, allowing him to have his mornings with his family and still make his desired income of $200,000 a year.

He lived each day finding moments to be grateful and happy. As he did this, job opportunities began to show up. But since he had a clear focus on what he wanted, he stayed the course of feeling as though the company with his dream job had already offered him a position.

He lived as though it had already happened.

Soon, the job of his dreams was offered and he took it gratefully. This job opened up the pathways for him to purchase both his home on the river and the SUV that took Sean and his family on many trips during which they created multiple memories. But these aren't the things that brought him fulfillment. . . .

The home, SUV, and trips *added* to the joy and happiness in Sean's life, but they weren't the root cause of them because his contentment came from a choice he made: the choice to **BE** (or feel) the way he really wanted to feel, FIRST. Sean had fully embraced the principle of **BE. DO. HAVE.** This is what allowed him to always feel the way he desired without having to *get* something to feel it. This cycle eliminates the overspending and indulgences that only bring you that temporary hit of happiness with an aftertaste of buyer's remorse.

The **BE. DO. HAVE.** model will allow you to attract more of what you want into your life. It is designed to help clear out the "when I get there, THEN I will feel _____" mindset.

The **HAVE. DO. BE.** model will lead you to burnout and unfilled expectations, leaving you always wanting and never truly getting what you want.

Now let's look at how you start to implement the **BE. DO. HAVE.** cycle.

- What is a desired feeling that you want to experience in your life (e.g., freedom, peace, relief, joy, excitement)?
- Are you willing to experiment and feel those feelings not because of an outside circumstance but simply because you choose to?
- How can you make these feelings and behaviors part of your daily life and routine? What can you start doing?

CREATE YOUR FREEDOM NOW

- What are you willing to stop doing? What boundary can you put in place to help with this (e.g., stop overworking, scarcity- and lack-thinking, or overspending)?

Remember, the subconscious will only give us what we believe we deserve. Loving yourself is essential to believing that money loves you.

Money Loves You Mindset Principle

Shift from HAVE. DO. BE. to BE. DO. HAVE.

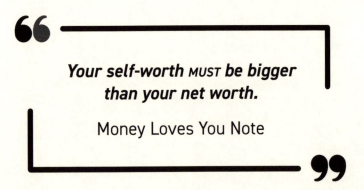

Your self-worth MUST *be bigger than your net worth.*

Money Loves You Note

CHAPTER TEN

SHATTER CONVENTIONAL RULES

Many personal finance experts love to tell you what to do with your money. They will give you (and shout to the world) the hard and fast rules that you "must follow" to achieve financial success—rules they say will eventually free you, as if their way is the only way that will work. And if you don't follow those rules, you will never be rich.

How does that feel? Does that leave you with a warm and fuzzy feeling? Or space to feel empowered and trusting you know what will be right for you?

I have noticed some clients want me to tell them exactly what to do while others want to be active participants in the process.

The truth is, some rules are meant to be broken. The more rules you place on money, the more it will be restricted. Embracing the *Money Loves You* mindset principles is shattering conventional rules about money and—here's the secret to finding *your* answers about money—trusting yourself and the wise counsel *you choose*.

Personal finance is exactly that: it's personal.

What if I shared that you can't do it wrong? There is no right or wrong way. There is no one-size-fits-all. There is not a good or bad way. It's not black and white.

Freedom is in the gray. **The gray is YOUR truth.**

Freedom equals truth and truth equals freedom.

You may not like this; you could be looking in this book for the exact formula to get rich and build wealth. But what I have noticed in those mindsets is that we are limiting ourselves. Trust yourself. *Rules* are there for when you don't trust yourself. But *boundaries* actually build self-trust and foster your ability to make choices based on your aspirations and desires.

Each one of us has different values, different priorities, and different standards. Boundaries make way more sense for our money.

This is what creates and maintains long-term financial freedom and independence. Boundaries won't make you want to rebel with that weekend shopping splurge or invest in some spur-of-the-moment opportunity.

Rules can lead to unhealthy behaviors, which is why I don't teach rules—because you will break them. And then you will once again find yourself stuck in the old patterns that got you here. Remember, "what got you here, won't get you THERE." What you have been doing up to this point in life with your finances has gotten you HERE. And I celebrate wherever you currently are. But I know it's not where you want to or could be. I know you have big aspirations for your money, so we must transform your actions to get you THERE.

Instead of using rules, I will guide you with boundaries. We want to create boundaries with our money because the boundaries give our money a place to go. Boundaries give direction and purpose. Just like the banks of a river create the boundaries for the water to create flow and direction, so will boundaries create flow and direction for your money.

In the next few chapters you will be learning the framework I call Inspired Wealth™. Remember, these are not rules you *must* follow. No, this is a framework that will help you direct your money and give it the boundaries it needs to fully produce and expand.

At the beginning of this book, I talked about having two true opposing thoughts or desires with your money at the same time. You might want to plan a lavish vacation to Europe *and* hit your financial savings goal. Both of those desires are the boundaries of the river. Some Financial Seasons™ will create a bend in the river toward your savings goal. Other Financial Seasons™ will be toward your European vacation. The river is of your own making. And, as water is a never ending-resource, so is money.

Over my career, I have noticed that clients love boundary conversations. They get to decide what is important to them as it relates to their money and then make the right decision for them.

As we have implemented the Inspired Wealth™ framework, I have watched knowledge and confidence grow exponentially for my clients and my personal life—because boundaries create safety. Likewise, your money begins to create safety and security for you and your family.

When you finish reading this book, I want you to feel empowered with your ability to make decisions that will impact your wealth in the most positive way possible.

Before and After Stories

Creating Freedom

Sarah is a strikingly beautiful brunette in her early fifties and she's a brilliant business executive. She makes good money and contributes to a retirement plan through her work. She is confident there will be sufficient savings for her future so she spends the rest of her money freely.

Sarah has three teenage daughters and one of their favorite activities is shopping. Most Saturdays, she loads up the girls in her Audi Q8 to go visit their favorite retailers and then treats them to lunch at their favorite sushi place. At times, Sarah feels irresponsible because she doesn't quite know how much money she is spending nor what she is teaching her girls. She does know they have a lot of fun and she enjoys nice things.

I met Sarah on a flight to New York, where we both were traveling for business. We sparked up a conversation about money when she noticed I was practicing and preparing to give a speech at a conference.

I shared with her the concepts of this book and she was specifically excited about the Value-based Cashflow™ method (see Chapter 14) and really looking at her spending through a new lens.

She joined our Inspired Wealth Platform™(see Chapter 11) and started working diligently with her financial coach to implement the tools. Within her first quarter she was able to pay off her credit card balance while still allocating money to enjoy shopping with her girls, and she decided to increase her non-retirement savings to invest for a vacation for the next year.

She shared with me the sense of freedom and empowerment she received from having boundaries with her money and being able to see all her progress on her Financial Empowerment Snapshot™(see Chapter 13). This framework has inspired her to intentionally build wealth and she is excited to be a positive example to her girls.

Houseless for a Life without Debt

The Johnson family had three children and an annual household income of $150,000. When they came to me for financial coaching and advice, they shared that they had read books on financial management and felt they needed to follow the rule that stated they must pay off their student loans before purchasing a home and investing.

For four years they worked tirelessly to pay off their student loans. During that time, they paid rent of $2,500 a month, which totaled $120,000 over the four years. So, instead of buying a home four years ago when the housing market was less expensive than it is now and having their $2500 a month pay a mortgage (and build equity), they paid that $2500 for rent and paid the same amount toward their student loans that they would have paid if they'd had a mortgage payment.

I asked them what was important to them. Did they enjoy renting and not having the obligation of a home to take care of? Did they want to wait until their student loan debt was paid off? What felt like the right decision to them?

The Johnsons shared that they would have loved to have bought a home. They said they could have purchased a new home with low maintenance for the same monthly payment as renting. They had even saved enough money to make a small down payment on a house but then read that was the wrong thing to do and that they should pay off the debt first.

Because they followed the "rule" that says you must pay off debt before you buy a home, they now have regrets. I shared that time is the greatest tool with our money. You can never get back time and it is a crucial part of building wealth.

I encouraged them by saying that they did the best they could with the information they had at the time. I inspired them to release this past decision and the feelings of regret, learn from the past decision, and move on by making different decisions in the future.

Once they understood their personal values and what the right decision was for them, they decided to start looking for their new home to purchase, even though they still owed $25,000 on their student loans.

The Life Not Lived

Paul loved following rules with his money. He had read every book he could find on finances and managing money. He prided himself on the fact that he had no debt and lived frugally. When his friends went out for dinner, he always declined and went home to eat dinner alone so he could save money. His savings account grew and he loved watching the numbers stack up. He never went on shopping sprees or bought extravagant items. His car was 15 years old and he loved being able to show that owning nice things wasn't a priority to him.

Then he met Molly, a free spirit who was beautiful and fun. She was totally different from him. He fell in love with the way she made him feel. Paul knew this was the girl he wanted to marry. At this point, he had saved over $200,000, had no debt, and lived way below his monthly income. Paul had the means to buy Molly the engagement ring of her dreams, but he lived by the rules—especially the rule that living frugally was wise. And so instead of buying her the one-carat square-diamond ring she had shown him, he purchased a ring with the smallest diamond they had in the store. He bought it with a sense of pride, knowing that he was following the rule and it would pay off.

Molly was disappointed and heartbroken when he popped the question with the small diamond ring that he had chosen. But she loved him, so she looked past the ring and focused on their life together.

As you can imagine, their honeymoon was a simple trip to the town next to theirs, instead of the dream trip to Hawaii they had both wanted.

The rules had definitely helped Paul create a savings account full of money. But the rules would deprive both of them of living a life filled with memories and dreams.

At first this method worked for them, but after 10 years of marriage and living with such financial confinement, resentment and frustration built up within their relationship. Because of the rules about money that Paul had brought to their relationship, Molly felt like she didn't have any say with money. She resented that Paul made all the decisions and she wasn't living the life she had always dreamed about. Molly could see that by this point, they had saved over a million dollars in their savings and investment accounts, but it was like a mirage: She could see it, but it felt as though it wasn't real.

This led to her wanting to rebel and go on wild shopping sprees. But, she feared what Paul would say if she did. So, she began her own business to make her own money so she could begin to live the life she wanted to live. Surprisingly, she was great at business and started to see money flow in. Because she had been so confined with money in her marriage, she spent money whenever she could. She would buy new clothes whenever she wanted and go on trips with girlfriends to see the places she had always wanted to see with Paul. But, since he couldn't let go of the rules that were dripping in shame and fear, she'd had to go on trips with her friends instead of with Paul. This led to even more resentment in their marriage and they were on the road to divorce.

This is when they found the Inspired Wealth Platform™. It was completely opposite of everything Paul had learned previously. He realized that what he had been doing might have grown his savings and investment accounts, but it wasn't working in his marriage.

The first thing the financial coach implemented with Paul and Molly was setting up their framework and getting them to agree to a monthly Money Loves You date (more on this in Chapter 16).

Within months their relationship went from disconnected, bitter, and resentful to connected with a clear focus on what they wanted to create in their life. Instead of rules confining them and constraining their relationship, they created Financial Seasons™ (explained in Chapter 15), which allowed them to focus on preparing for a dream vacation together while also investing in their future.

SHATTER CONVENTIONAL RULES

The framework met both of their needs because they threw out rules and built boundaries based on their desires.

Soon their relationship was stronger than ever and not only were they learning how to invest their money so that it was growing for them but they began to truly live life and invest in memories as well.

Where in your life have you focused on the rules, only to miss out on what was really important? Rules keep you captive and don't require your input. Rules can make you numb and block critical thinking; they shut down your access to your superconscious powers.

The beauty of boundaries is they belong to us and we get to establish them. We decide what our boundaries are based on our desires, our values, and our truth.

As you approach the tools in this book to help you build your framework with money, remember that you are in charge. No one knows your situation and every one of us is unique. I encourage you to feel empowered to make the money choices that are right for your path.

Money Loves You Mindset Principle

Personal finance is exactly that: it's personal.

You can't do it wrong. There is no right or wrong way.
There is no one-size-fits-all. There is not a good or bad way.
It's not black and white.

Freedom is in the gray. The gray is YOUR truth. Freedom equals truth and truth equals freedom.

MONEY LOVES YOU NOTE

CHAPTER ELEVEN

INSPIRED WEALTH™

This is the chapter you have been waiting for since you started your financial journey. I know that's a bold statement. Here's the good news: I have over 27 years of proof that shows I know that what I am about to teach you will free you from the old, constraining ways. This will liberate and empower you to discover new ways of creating, growing, and maintaining financial wealth.

The first 10 chapters and the effort you put in thus far have set you up to now take inspired action with practical tools you can implement with your money. In the next several chapters you are going to dive deeper and begin doing the work of designing your path to financial independence and start working with the Inspired Wealth™ framework.

Financial freedom can happen in an instant; it's yours the moment you decide to create a plan and take inspired action toward your financial aspirations.

Your path will not be perfect and it's not meant to be. Your inspired wealth journey will have twists and turns, unexpected exits, and even U-turns.

The question is: *do you have room for all of the abundance ahead and are you ready to experience true financial freedom, increased confidence, and financial success?*

Think of your financial potential as an overstuffed closet. Let me paint you a visual. For years, I struggled with cleaning out my closet. I just couldn't bring myself to get rid of clothes or shoes that I had spent good money on. I also enjoy getting new shoes and clothes and I just kept adding without getting rid of anything and the situation was getting out of hand. I had no more room for new clothes and I was stuck trying to figure out how to purge. I eventually hired a stylist coach to help me (yes, it got this bad!).

She encouraged me to ask myself, *Why can't I let this go? What is holding me hostage to this stuff?* I couldn't possibly wear it all. I was overwhelmed with all the baggage. A whole section of clothes in my closet didn't fit me anymore—they were from my crazy bodybuilding days when I weighed 20 pounds less than I do now.

Subconsciously, I was hoping that one day I would be back to that size. When I thought about this consciously, I realized that was just not a way I wanted to care for and love my body. I am not willing to put my body through so many unhealthy efforts to go back to that place. I value vitality and energy way more than being a size four.

Similar to the experience of my unhealthy bodybuilding efforts and the resulting loss of vitality, sometimes people feel they need to be so sacrificial *today* for their future financial goals that they rob themselves of current opportunities to have meaningful experiences and make memories.

My stylist worked with me to define my personal style and gave me guidelines for how to go through my wardrobe. She helped me reframe my thoughts of *maybe someday I'll wear this* and was incredibly helpful with my mindset. Ever so gently, she recommended I set a timer for 20 minutes and then see what I could easily say "no" to. I started throwing things into a pile—all the clothes that didn't fit me, all the clothes that didn't bring me joy when I wore them, all the gifts I had received that weren't really my style—and after the 20-minute timer sounded, I kept going. Over the course of a weekend, not only had I purged 10 bags from my closet and felt like a new person but I went on to clear other clutter piles throughout my home. I cleared out many versions of myself, someone I no longer was. This was incredibly freeing for me.

When I took the clutter out of my closet and home, I could see the things that I loved. I felt content and happy. I didn't have the desire for more.

The next week I took the bags to Goodwill. As I took each bag out of my car and handed it over, I noticed I had the biggest smile on my face and felt like a weight was being lifted off me.

Over the course of the next two months, without effort or thought, I lost 10 pounds. I felt excited to go into my closet each morning, knowing that what I was looking at in my closet, I loved. I also had a heightened sense of self-love as I finally took the time to clear out the clutter.

Cleaning out my closet and home created space for *new*. I look back now and see the new people, ideas, and opportunities that have come into my life since then. This book is a result of cleaning out my clutter, letting go of the old stories, and being inspired to get creative to share new ways to work with money.

I want to help you clean out your financial closet so that you have MORE room for your desired results! When we let go of what no longer "fits" us, we make room for new goals and dreams to come in.

We can get caught up in thinking we should ask for only what we think we *should* have or what we *deserve* and not leave room for wonder and miracles. I encourage you to ask for MORE. Make room for MORE. Prepare yourself to receive MORE and get rid of what doesn't serve you—your thoughts, the things you feel obligated to keep, and the clutter piles in your office, your kitchen, and even in your head.

Having a mentality of lack and scarcity attracts lack and scarcity. The avoidance of money makes money avoid you. The fear of not having enough or the fear of having too much will repel money and leave you struggling.

We must guard our hearts and minds with diligence, knowing we attract back to us the energy we put out into the world. I can feel your question: *so how do I shift out of the fear and scarcity state I am in with my money?* We do this by simply doing the work—all that was in the previous chapters combined with a powerful framework that is coming your way.

The Inspired Wealth™ framework is the path that will take you to the life you dream of with your money. This is completely different from anything that is currently being taught, which means it might feel foreign at times. I invite you to welcome the changes and resistance. Because remember, what got you here won't get you where you want to go, and that means you'll have to be willing to change things up!

The tools in the Inspired Wealth ™ framework will be that change for you. And the best part is . . . these tools are created to be unique to YOU.

Have you ever noticed the difference between being a passenger in a bus versus being the driver in your car? If you are the passenger, it is very likely that you don't remember the route you took to your destination. Maybe you were on your phone, distracted, or deep in conversation and not paying attention to the landmarks or even the direction you were headed. But as the driver, you are very aware of the current location and the direction you are going and maybe even taking note of all the landmarks along the way. You would most likely be able to return to your starting point with ease because of your awareness during the drive there.

Many times when we hire a financial advisor or delegate our finances solely to our partner, they are in the driver's seat and we take on the role of a passive passenger. This is great if you never want to drive the car. But, if you ever quit working with that advisor, or find yourself suddenly single, you will feel lost and hindered by not being able to continue on your desired path.

I have noticed a shift in our clients from wanting us, as advisors, to drive the car to wanting us to sit beside them to help them navigate their course and to guide them away from danger. I think of my role as being an active passenger providing the navigation. The next generation of investors wants a more active coaching relationship with their advisor—a relationship that is collaborative and empowering.

I believe in empowering you with your money. I do promote finding the right financial coach and advisor, like those on my Inspired Wealth Platform™, to help support you on your financial journey. But I want YOU to be the driver. I want you to understand where you are going and how you are getting there. If you understand the roadmap, you will never get lost and will arrive where you intend to go.

Over the next five chapters I will guide you through using and implementing the Inspired Wealth™ framework and tools. These include:

- **Freedom Number™**
- **Financial Empowerment Snapshot™**
- **Value-based Cashflow™**
- **Financial Seasons™**
- **Money Loves You, Relationship-building Process™**

Each one builds on the other and each is also powerful as a stand-alone tool. By completing the steps in these chapters, you take everything you have learned thus far and put it into action.

You have probably gone through many different paths on your financial journey. Some of them may have been wild successes while others may have felt hard and frustrating. Or maybe you may have been stuck on one path that just isn't working in your best interest. I admire you for choosing to be here now. I acknowledge you for trying something new and different to create long-lasting wealth. And I don't take lightly that I am a guide for you as you step into the unknown.

I invite you to trust me. Trust that the Inspired Wealth™ framework will give you the tools you need to become secure in your money and allow you to experience the growth ahead.

Money Loves You Mindset Principle

We must guard our hearts and our minds with diligence, knowing we attract back to us the energy we put out into the world.

Financial freedom can happen in an instant; it's yours the moment you decide to create a plan and take inspired action toward your financial aspirations.

MONEY LOVES YOU NOTE

CHAPTER TWELVE

FREEDOM NUMBER™

Imagine yourself 10 years from now. What does your life look like? How has it changed? Where do you live? What is your income level? How has your lifestyle changed? How have you spent the last 10 years?

Really, please take a few minutes to close your eyes and visualize where you hope to be in 10 years. This vision can be your reality *if* you imagine it vividly and make decisions *today* that are based on what you want in the future.

In this chapter, I will guide you through how you can make that future vision a reality by setting your personal Freedom Number™. This number allows you to focus on what you want in the future. It will also help you to eliminate many (or all) of the "how" questions that come up in your mind that try to trick you into believing that number is impossible.

Studies indicate that individuals who establish a strong connection to their "future selves" are more likely to make financial choices that benefit them in the long run.

You can enhance this connection by vividly and authentically envisioning yourself in the future. In doing this, the stronger connection to your future self leads to actions that can help secure financial well-being in the years to come.

Over the past year I have had the honor of working with Dr. Benjamin Hardy, author of, *Be Your Future Self Now*. I also visited the UCLA Anderson School of Management and studied with Professor Hal Hershfield, who wrote, *Your Future Self*. I highly recommend both books.

Hershfield's book, *Your Future Self*, is about how we can influence our choices today by thinking about our life in the future. He shares that while we obviously want the best possible future for ourselves, we often fail to make decisions that would truly make our desired future self a reality. He reveals why it's often hard to think about the future when we are making decisions now.

For example, why do we choose the pasta, bread, and dessert at the restaurant instead of fish and vegetables, which would support our decision to lose weight? Why do we splurge on luxury cars rather than save and invest for our future? Why do we hit the snooze button and keep sleeping when we just committed to a new morning workout routine?

Dr. Hershfield has researched and studied this for over a decade and explains in his book that in our minds, our future selves often look like strangers. In his book, Hershfield teaches us that if we can connect with the person we want to become, we will be better able to integrate living for today with sticking to our commitments in planning for tomorrow.

Working with Dr. Benjamin Hardy has transformed my thinking about my future self and what's possible. People who have achieved the biggest aspirations of their heart start by envisioning their goals and desires in their minds. They dare to dream an impossible vision they have for themselves and while holding onto that vision, they work toward it. As they take steps forward, their ideas become clearer, then bigger, and then reality.

The real challenge for us is to take the time to sharpen the picture of our financial future and act upon that picture. What we see in our future should inspire us to take action. If you don't feel inspired, take the time to create a future that does. Take a moment to picture your future self. Do you see a financial future for yourself that hasn't changed in awhile? What if you were to choose a different financial future? What if you could commit to what you really, truly desire?

FREEDOM NUMBER™

When you wholeheartedly commit to your desires and believe that you will achieve them, you'll start to see evidence of the future you're creating. The hard work you do and changes you need to make to reach your goals won't feel painful anymore. Instead, the pain would come from not making progress toward your dreams.

Learning from Dr. Benjamin Hardy and Professor Hal Hershfield has inspired me to think about this future-self concept with money. What if I could help people define their future financial life, quantify that into a number, then bring that back to them today? Would that inspire them with their money choices? Would they make different decisions, knowing these daily habits will take them to their desired future financial-self?

Would this pull them into the future and keep their focus? I know it's kept my focus all these years. I realized this is exactly what I've been doing with my personal finances and it's what we've done with our clients. We all need ongoing motivation and inspiration as we stay committed to our future financial selves.

Freedom Number™ Tool

The first step in finding your Freedom Number™ is totaling your current household monthly income.

This current income number is powerful because it's what you have been trusted with at this stage in your life. We have learned that the principle of being trusted with little turns into being trusted with much. The responsibility over this amount of monthly income will be the magnet that attracts more.

Let's take a look at your number. How do you feel about it?

_____

_____

Current Monthly Income? _____

Do you want it to be more? How much more? _____

Future Financial-Self (FFS) Monthly Income? _____

At this point, don't worry about how you will make this amount of money. Trust that when the vision is clear, the "how" takes care of itself.

Future Financial-Self (FFS) Annual Income Calculation:

FFS Monthly Income _____ X 12 = FFS Annual Income: _____

Next, I want to ensure you understand what financial independence is. Financial independence is achieved when your assets create enough income for you to cover the lifestyle you want without needing to generate income from your own efforts (like going to work).

There is no magic number for financial independence because everyone is unique. I have created a simple formula to help you get a general idea of how much you'll need in order to have the yearly income you want for your future self.

Freedom Number™ Calculation:

FFS Annual Income _____ x 30 = Your Freedom Number™

This is YOUR financial independence number. THIS is your FREEDOM Number™.

This can be a lofty tool that is often overlooked but let me share with you my experience.

In 2010, my personal annual income was $100,000. When I thought about the future, I remember wanting to make $250,000 and, based on my future financial-self projections, this felt like a good number. Here is what it looks like with the formula:

$250,000 Future Financial-Self Annual Income Goal

$250,000 X 30 = $7,500,000—this would create financial independence for my family. THIS is my Freedom Number™.

These two numbers become my future financial-self inspiration. When you quantify your future financial goals and put them in writing, the subconscious can go to work on it for you. I am amazed as I see this play out in my life over and over again.

Beware! This is your baseline and will evolve and change over time as you move along your financial journey. With more income and assets come more responsibilities and things to consider. This formula is by no means a financial plan; rather, it is a tool that provides something to work toward.

FREEDOM NUMBER™

A factor of 30 projects a conservative rate of return and the impact of inflation over the long term.

As you build wealth, it's important to work with a financial professional who can develop a proactive tax plan, think through estate-planning techniques in line with your values, and help with many other things. These are advanced strategies that a trusted financial advisor can help you with but are not the intention and focus of this book.

Your Freedom Number™ is a gift to your current self. This number represents what your future self gets to experience. Imagine this as the best time-travel gift that never ends. Knowing this number will allow you to make decisions now that will affect your future self.

Most humans don't think that far into their future. There exists some sense of not belonging to your own future. Many feel like their future self will just know how to make more money and take care of itself. This creates the excuse that you don't need to worry about your future right now.

Often, our present-day finances are so intense that our future self does not feel like a priority. The truth is, no one is coming to save you . . . but YOU.

I know that may sound harsh, but it's the reality. Many live their lives acting as though something amazing is going to happen and their future will be set. This might sound like, "When my employer finally goes public, all of my shares will be worth thousands of dollars," or "When my inheritance money comes in, I will be set." Possibly it is the dream of that huge raise or the sale of your home.

Now, all of these things can very well happen. Your employer might go public. Or it might never go public and the years relying on that dream will only leave you with what you currently have and no sturdy future to lean on.

Your inheritance money most likely will come through, unless there has been a medical emergency and the relative you are hoping to receive the inheritance from uses all of that money.

I believe good things are coming to you and more will come to you *if* you create a future for yourself based on your own actions. If all of the other things come through, then you will have more than enough.

When you rely on circumstances that are not within your control to set you up for success in the future, you will most likely end up disappointed and ill-prepared.

Focusing on your Freedom Number™ is what creates success now and for your future self.

There will most likely be distractions as you try to create the time to be with your future financial-self. Distractions such as family drama, work chaos, bills, and unmet needs will get your attention. Notice them but don't let them take you off course. Maintain your focus and your life will be blessed now and in the future to come.

I believe you can access the wisdom of your future self through your superconscious mind simply by taking time for reflection and visualization. In the section below, I have created a "Meet Your Future Financial-Self Visualization" to support you through that experience.

If this is a hard concept for you to swallow, that's okay. A simple way to understand this is to imagine the version of who you are today, then go back to who you were 10 years ago. What life lessons would you teach that version of you that would have helped you dodge some serious struggles? What good advice would you give you that would set you up for success?

That is what we are doing with your future self right now. Except YOU are the past version and are receiving wisdom from the future version of you. This practice will aid you in making wiser decisions that, in the long-run, affect your future life.

If you would like to be guided through this visualization, use this QR code to listen.

FREEDOM NUMBER™

Meet Your Future Financial-Self Visualization

Find a quiet and comfortable space where you can relax. As you embark on this future financial-self reflection and visualization, open your mind to the possibilities of your future financial-self. Set aside any preconceived notions or judgments and allow your imagination to take you on this journey.

Close your eyes and begin taking a couple deep breaths, inhaling through the nose, holding for a couple seconds, and then exhaling slowly through your mouth. With each breath, let go of any tension or stress, allowing yourself to become more and more relaxed. Let external sounds serve as a reminder to leave the outside world behind and enter the serene realm of your inner world.

Imagine a large root of a beautiful old-growth tree extending down from the base of your spine deep into the earth, anchoring and tethering you to the center of the earth. No matter where your inner journey and imagination takes you, this connection keeps you solidly rooted.

As you sink into a deeper state of relaxation, visualize yourself standing before a magnificent and peaceful lake. Take in the tranquility of the surroundings. Notice if the water is a shade of blue or green or a combination of both. Observe the small waves as they gently move against the shoreline, coming in and peacefully going out. Envision your body as this body of water, and with each thought of your future financial-self, send ripples of positive change throughout your being.

Pause for a moment and feel the waves of relaxation flowing through your entire body, from your head to your toes. As your muscles release tension, you become more serene and at ease.

Now, direct your attention to the space between your eyes, often referred to as the third eye or your mind's eye. Visualize a deep-blue or indigo-colored light. Breathe.

Pause.

Let this light transform into your preferred mode of transportation—whether it's a car, a boat, a plane, a helicopter, or perhaps even a spaceship. Step into the vehicle, buckle up, and take off. As you find yourself traveling at the speed of light well into the future, specifically 10 years ahead, you instantly arrive at your destination in the future.

Pause.

Take note of where you land; this is where your future financial-self resides. Step into this future realm and take in your surroundings. What does your future home look like?

What natural elements surround it—trees, flowers, water, or other features? Pay attention to colors, light, and textures.

Stand before your future home and invite someone to come to the door. Behind that door is your future financial-self, welcoming you into the world of 10 years from now. Observe your future financial-self's appearance, posture, and attire. Sense their energy and well-being.

Pause.

Take a moment to explore the interior of your future home. Who else resides here? What is the home like? Are there others present, and if so, what are they like?

Pause.

Move to a comfortable place for a conversation with your future financial-self. Make yourself comfortable for this dialogue.

Start thinking about what questions you would love to ask your future self. To get you started, begin with these two fundamental questions:

> *"What do you most remember about the last 10 years, Future Self?"*
> *"What is the most important lesson to share with me?"*

Take a moment to listen to their response.

Pause.

Now, ask your future financial-self, "What do I need to know that will help me become you in the future? What insights can guide me on this financial journey?" Listen attentively to their wisdom.

Pause.

Feel free to ask your future financial-self any other questions that come to mind. Take a moment to inquire about your specific financial goals and aspirations.

Pause.

Before concluding your visit, ask your future financial-self one final question: "What gift do you have for me?" The gift will be something that symbolizes your future financial-self that will serve as inspiration on your journey.

Pay attention to any words, images, or gifts that arise as you listen to their answer.

FREEDOM NUMBER™

Pause.

Express your gratitude to your future financial-self for sharing their wisdom with you today. Acknowledge that you can return to this visualization whenever you desire.

Say your goodbyes.

Now, find your way back to the vehicle that brought you to your future and journey back up into space. Watch the world of 10 years into the future shrink as you return to the present. Observe the Earth below as you descend, and when you reach your current time and location, re-enter the room where you began.

Take a few moments to bask in the experience you've just had. Draw your attention back to the earth and feel it beneath you, grounding you in this present moment. Continue to breathe as you start wiggling your fingers and toes, stretching your body. When you feel ready, open your eyes. As you do, remain silent and take notes on the insights and visions you've experienced.

How was that?

_____

_____

What were the answers to your questions?

_____

_____

What gift or special message did you receive?

_____

_____

What did your superconscious share with you during the visualization?

_____

_____

Choose now to make the decisions that will affect your future self. In the next chapter, I will guide you through the next Inspired Wealth™ tool: Financial Empowerment Snapshot™. This is an empowering tool that will help you see the truth and pull you into your future financial-self.

Scan this QR code to access additional resources provided by Professor Hal Hershfield. These resources will help you stay on track to become the financial self you've visualized for your future.

Money Loves You Mindset Principle

What we see in our future drives us to take action.

Your Freedom Number™ is a gift to your current self. This number represents what your future self gets to experience. Imagine this as the best time-travel gift that never ends.

Our present-day finances are so intense that our future self does not feel like a priority. The truth is, no one is coming to save you . . . but YOU.

MONEY LOVES YOU NOTE

CHAPTER THIRTEEN

SEE TRUTH

My hope is that, by now, you have excitement and desire to build wealth and you are feeling inspired to start taking action. This is where action begins—with a burning desire to change and want something different for your future—to be empowered and have a willingness to look in the financial mirror.

A desire is a strong wish or wanting to have something—something you don't have today—that is going to require a change. What do you desire? Could it be financial independence, becoming debt-free, buying a second home, or traveling the world? You get to decide what it is for you. And this is where people get stuck. People want all the things—the new home, investment account, new car, new boat, tropical vacation—all at the same time, and that isn't how it works.

I like to say, you can have all the things, just not all at the same time. Desires take time to manifest and this is actually what makes them rewarding. As you follow this framework, build wealth, and achieve goals, you will see the momentum build and things can change quickly. This is because you are evolving personally. Who you become in the process of getting your life's desires is the fuel that keeps the momentum going.

In order to change our behavior we need to acknowledge our desires. Thus, it is important to understand and find your "why" behind the desire. Understanding "why" is the most important type of knowledge because it helps us figure out *what* to do and *how* to do it. For example, if we know why the stock market goes up and down, we can make better decisions about investing.

Let's say you have a strong desire to improve your financial situation. You want to save money, invest wisely, and achieve financial stability. This desire may have various motivations behind it, but to truly understand your "why," you need to dig deeper.

Your "why" might be rooted in the desire to provide a better life for your family. You want to ensure that your children have access to quality education and opportunities that you may not have had. This sense of responsibility and love for your family serves as your primary motivation.

Understanding your "why" is crucial because it not only clarifies your goals but also guides your actions. When faced with the temptation to spend money impulsively or deviate from your financial plan, reminding yourself of the "why"—the well-being and future prospects of your family—can provide the emotional strength and determination you need to stay on track.

In this example, the "why" is the emotional and personal reason behind your desire to change your financial behavior. It gives you a powerful incentive and a constant reminder of your ultimate goal, making it easier to implement the necessary sacrifices and decisions to achieve financial stability. Whatever your desire is, the "why" needs to pull you into making a decision and committing to yourself.

When desire is followed with a decision it means you are committed to changing and willing to cut off all other options so you can move forward. A decision leads to action and dedication, which require courageous determination toward the commitment you have made to yourself.

When we don't follow a framework or have boundaries with our money, decision fatigue can easily set in. Decision fatigue is real and happens when we need to make too many decisions in life.

For example, how many of us, after a long day at work, come home with plans to make a healthy dinner at home but the kids or spouse say, "Let's go out to eat." With no willpower left in you, you say "okay" and go out to dinner.

This happens in all aspects of our lives because we have no decision-making ability left. When we have to make too many decisions, we have no energy left to make good or wise ones.

One easy way to see decision fatigue is in the process of purchasing a new car. If you don't know what you want or are looking for, the hundreds of different options become overwhelming. Soon, you feel exhausted by everything that is available. This leads you to either buying any car simply because you are tired of looking or leaving empty-handed because the decision fatigue was too much. But if you know what you want, the experience is quick and simple. They either have what you are looking for, or they don't. You leave with the car of your choice, or they will contact you when they find it. Decision fatigue leads to poor choices and undesirable results.

When "everything" is an option, it is easy to get tired of making decisions and inevitably falling into old default thinking. Your old default thinking takes us back to Chapter 7 and those nasty Wealth Busters that lead you back into the unlucky cycles with money and the old ruts.

Establishing your boundaries and implementing the Inspired Wealth™ framework creates the discipline and focus that make the decisions for you. This is also how you will continue to build trust with yourself and with your money-making decisions.

It takes courage to implant new thoughts in your mind and experience new feelings as you embody your future financial-self. This ultimately leads you to taking new actions toward your desired outcome. The rewards of this cycle are confidence and freedom. It may feel daunting and unknown, but that is why I am here to guide you through this process—so you can pursue the confidence and freedom that is available to you.

But before we can get to the rewards of financial confidence and freedom, *we must be willing to see the truth and look into our financial mirror.* We all know what it is like to look in the mirror and not see the image we want. However, we are the ones who hold the power to transform it.

Let me tell you a short story about my friend Ruth. She has five kids and is a small-business owner. When 2020 hit, not only did she have to pivot with how she ran business but she also became a full-time teacher when she was forced to homeschool all five of her kids.

During this stressful time, she noticed that none of her clothes fit anymore. Ruth didn't own a full-length mirror or a scale and didn't have the time to worry about her small weight gain, so she continued on with her lifestyle. Until one day, she saw a picture of herself and barely recognized herself. Ruth decided that she needed outside support for her physical health. She joined a weight-loss platform that had individual coaches. The first thing she was coached to do was to buy a full length mirror and scale. It was time for her to see the truth of her situation.

When she stepped on the scale, she was floored to see that she had gained 40 pounds during the pandemic. Since she never saw herself or checked her weight, it had spiraled out of control.

After having compassion for herself and realizing the stress she had been under with homeschooling five kids and restructuring her business, it was time to take action to regain her full health.

But this couldn't happen until Ruth stepped on the scale and began seeing herself daily in the mirror.

Ruth needed to see the truth about her weight gain and have a clear focus on her goal. After hiring the coaches necessary to help her stay accountable to her health aspirations, Ruth lost all her extra weight in two years' time. She now feels amazing and has become an inspiration to her children. Ruth has taught them that anything is possible when you see the truth, have focus, and reach out for support!

This book isn't about weight loss, but the story lends itself to our financial situations.

If you want to be in your highest financial health, you must first be willing to see the truth.

All financial progress begins by looking into the financial mirror.

Be willing to see the truth. This is where many other financial experts will start to use shame and guilt. They do this to try to corral you into a corner and hope you will make better decisions with your money from then on. This tactic is an old model that doesn't serve you or your wealth. Notice that as you go through this tool with me, you might experience old feelings of shame or regret. Just notice them as old learned behaviors and then let them go. They are not going to serve you or your wealth.

Just like Ruth felt compassion for her weight gain, you too have the opportunity to feel compassion for yourself as you begin to see the truth of your financial health. I am going to guide you through this tool without shame, fear, or blame. Instead, we will be going through it with love.

Money begins to come alive when you pay attention to it. Remember, money takes on our emotions, words, thoughts, beliefs, and identity.

I help my clients see their financial truth and build wealth by using the next Inspired Wealth™ tool: the Financial Empowerment Snapshot™. If you have never looked at your full financial picture on one page this could either be exciting and empowering or depressing and debilitating. No matter where you fall on the spectrum of emotions, I am right here with you. I have seen it all and no matter where you start, it's not the end of the story.

Allow the truth to set you free; it might be uncomfortable or even painful at first, but it will set you free.

The Financial Empowerment Snapshot™ is a work-in-progress document. It is a tool that captures the current picture of your financial mirror. Note: this is a tool, not a shaming device! The first time you complete this tool it's simply a starting point, like your before picture.

Instructions for Financial Empowerment Snapshot™

Start on the left-hand side of the worksheet and list your assets. Your assets are what you own. This could be money in the bank, your car, your home, rental real estate property, a business you own, investment accounts, 401(k), other retirement accounts, stocks, and bonds. I have listed the most commonly reported assets to get you started. If you don't have these, no problem, just put in zero.

You'll notice on the worksheet is a place for liquid assets. This is money that can be accessed easily, including your money in the bank, your investment accounts—anything you could liquidate and get cash for relatively quickly. Do not include your real estate or car in this area. It is good to keep track of this separately to ensure you are building liquid assets.

Next, we need to identify your liabilities. Your liabilities are any debt you owe. This could be a mortgage on your home or a home-equity line of credit. This also includes consumer debt like auto loans, RV loans, medical bills, credit cards, store credit cards, and student loans.

Please list all liabilities owed and write those on the right side of the worksheet. Again, I have listed the most common liabilities to get you started.

Once you complete the list, you will have one column for your assets and one column for your liabilities. Your net worth, then, is the total of your assets minus the total of your liabilities.

SEE TRUTH

MONEY LOVES YOU TOOL

Financial Empowerment Snapshot™

Date: _____

Assets	Amount ($)	Liabilities	Amount ($)
Liquid and Retirement Account Assets			
Bank Savings	$	Mortgage	$
Money Market	$	Other Home Equity Loan	$
Certificate of Deposit (CD)	$	Rental Real Estate Mortgage	$
Investment Account	$	Car	$
Stock	$	Vehicle Other	$
Savings Bonds	$	RV	$
ROTH IRA #1	$	Credit Card	$
ROTH IRA #2	$	Student Loan	$
Traditional IRA #1	$	Other:	$
Traditional IRA #2	$	Other:	$
401k or Employer-Sponsored Plan #1	$	Other:	$
401k or Employer-Sponsored Plan #2	$		
Custodian Account Child #1	$		
Custodian Account Child #2	$		
529 or Other College Savings Account	$		
Other:	$		
Other:	$		
Other:	$		
Other Assets			
Primary Home	$		
Secondary Home	$		
Rental Real Estate	$		
Other Real Estate	$		
Car	$		
Truck	$		
RV	$		
Other	$		
Other	$		
Other	$		
Total Other Assets	$		
Total Assets	$	**Total Liabilities**	$
Net Worth	$		

The Formula:
Total Assets - Total Liabilities = Net Worth

Download Free Financial Empowerment Snapshot™ PDF

This exercise brings awareness and is a great way to understand what your financial picture looks like today. Remember, this is just your first version.

If your Financial Empowerment Snapshot™ shows a negative net worth, it's okay; just acknowledge it and move forward—no guilt, excuses, anxiety, blame, or despair. Spending time dwelling on these negative feelings creates more of the same results and isn't going to elicit real change. Your desire—your "why" rooted in love—is the driver of change. Just think of how much of a success story yours will be one, three, and five years from now. You will be thankful you saved this first version.

I completed my first version of this in 2005 and I am blown away at how I have seen our Financial Empowerment Snapshot™ change over the years. I would encourage you to keep all your versions because they will serve as inspiration for what is possible and what you have achieved.

This is the most powerful component of your Inspired Wealth™ journey; I have also found it's the hardest. As you move forward, the rest will be easier. I can say that from experience with the many people I've worked with, as well as from personal experience. You have done the hard work and the momentum is yours. Allow it to pull you into your desired future.

Money Loves You Mindset Principle

Establishing your boundaries and implementing the Inspired Wealth™ framework creates the discipline and focus that make the decisions for you.

What you track improves. Whatever you track and report improves exponentially.

MONEY LOVES YOU NOTE

CHAPTER FOURTEEN

WELCOME TO THE ANTI-BUDGET!

Where your focus goes, your energy flows. Which means . . . if you are avoiding your money, money will avoid you. If you take care of your money, your money takes care of you.

Most money books will put too much emphasis on budgeting, which doesn't work. How do I know it doesn't work? Because most of my clients hate budgets and have a negative gut reaction to budgeting. You probably hate budgets. I hate budgets. So why do we keep trying to teach a model that DOESN'T work? We have evolved as humans. We don't want to be told what to do. We don't want to be confined or restricted.

Trying to budget and control your spending and allocate every penny puts an obsessive attention and restriction on your money. Yes, it's helpful to track your money and know where it goes, but it's better done with loving intention and excitement for spending money the way you want and on things you value.

When I have tried, and also witnessed my clients try, to follow a complex budgeting system, a common experience is to fall behind with it (because of not having enough time to devote to it), feel defeated, and quit.

As I was doing research for this book, I gathered feedback from clients and the public. Guess what the #1 desire was from 98% of the responses: FREEDOM.

Almost every person who filled out this survey said they wanted freedom. While discipline with our money creates freedom, most people find that traditional budgeting creates confinements and contention in their lives.

Here are a few reasons why:

- Budgeting focuses on restriction and tightening. What you focus on expands.
- Budgeting is like a diet, which creates a binge experience. Filled with rigidity, shame, and restraint, it leads to the unconscious behavior to break the rules.
- If budgeting creates stress, you will AVOID budgeting. Avoidance is where you can get stuck.

Instead of restricting you . . . I want to FREE you! I don't want you to feel like your budget has power over you. I want you to feel EMPOWERED with your money choices. I want you to be in charge of your money instead of being controlled by your money.

Freedom with your money doesn't mean you don't pay attention to how you spend it. I have created the Value-based Cashflow™ method. It is the anti-budget tool that will FREE you, create room for ABUNDANCE, and leave you empowered and disciplined with your money.

Instead of an energy of restriction and the lack mentality that budgets often make us feel, the Value-based Cashflow™ method is designed to align your spending habits with your values and leave you with a sense of freedom. The only way to get to freedom is through discipline. Freedom is found in the discipline of boundaries and ensuring you are spending your money on things that genuinely matter to you.

The anti-budget Value-based Cashflow™ method is about understanding your values and goals, examining your spending patterns, and being empowered to identify whether or not your expenses align with your values. Understanding your money values provides a foundation for making intentional and informed financial decisions.

WELCOME TO THE ANTI-BUDGET!

Tracking and paying attention to your money is critical to making progress toward your financial goals. Equally as important is understanding what your core values are and how they influence your financial decisions. For example, if family is important to you, you may prioritize spending on activities that strengthen family bonds.

Let me guide you through this anti-budget method that brings you clarity, focus, and energy. When it comes to your monthly cash flow, remember: money loves to be in motion. It's meant to flow in both directions. Embrace this! You should never feel bad or guilty about spending money.

Instead, I want you to feel excited about spending it *intentionally* on things that genuinely contribute to your well-being and happiness. Understanding your money values enables you to make intentional decisions about where your money goes each month and ensure you are spending it on what you love and value and what will serve the life you envision for your future.

The first step is to understand what you value most about money by looking at your spending habits. I want you to go now—like *right now*, as you are reading this—and open your bank account activity or your last credit card statement, or both. Look at how you spent your money in the last 30 days. As you examine your account activity you'll discover three general types of relationships you have with your purchases and expenses:

- **Joy**
- **Comfort**
- **Annoyance**

Let's start with joy. As you look at your account activity, what purchase or expenses brought you the most joy? It could be your house payment because you are building equity in your home. It could be the cost of your appointment with an acupuncturist or massage therapist that provided you much-needed self-care. Or maybe it was dinner out with your kids when they came home from college for a short visit. I know I love to see the money leave our checking account each month and go into our investments or to a payment for an upcoming vacation.

MONEY LOVES YOU

In the space below, write down which purchases or expenses brought you the most joy. What did you love to spend money on?

_____

_____

We all have expenses each month that are just part of life and can't be avoided. These expenses, although mundane, create comfort for us. I challenge you to see these expenses with a new lens.

Here are a few examples of expenses that may be mundane costs but how we view them can foster positive emotion:

- **Gas**: I'm grateful it fuels my car and gives me freedom to go places.
- **Electricity**: I love having lights on in my house so I can read my favorite books.
- **Car payment**: I'm happy to have dependable transportation for my family and me and knowing I am making progress on paying off my debt.
- **Water bill**: It is so convenient to have running water in my home. I am so thankful I can run my washing machine and dishwasher to keep my household in order. I love being able to turn on faucets and have warm showers.
- **Health and car insurance**: It brings such peace of mind knowing that my family has health insurance when someone is sick or needs medical attention. Or, if I'm ever in a car accident, I know insurance will cover repairs to my car.
- **Groceries**: I am so grateful that I can buy healthy food for my family and me.

Take some time now to write out your comfort expenses:

_____

_____

_____

Lastly, do you see anything in your activity history that makes you feel regret, annoyed, guilty, or mad? Was this a necessary expense? Can you get

WELCOME TO THE ANTI-BUDGET!

rid of a cost like this in the future or rewire your mindset to think about it in a positive way?

Here are a few examples of expenses that could make you feel negative emotions:

- **Impulse purchases**: I don't know about you but there are times when I leave Costco, Target, or Walmart (or any big box retailer) and say what the heck did I just spend $350 on?
- **Consistent overindulgences**: We are all different but this could be daily coffee runs, happy-hour drinks, or ordering takeout daily for lunch and dinner. I think we can all decide what it is for us that we could remove from our spending that would allow us to make progress on our financial goals.

Write down the expenses you have spent money on in the last 30 days that you wish you hadn't or feel annoyed by.

_____

_____

_____

Ask yourself, what can I **stop spending money on** so I can redirect these funds to the things I do value and that bring me joy, including building a secure financial future? These are the costs to eliminate to increase money to invest in your future.

_____

_____

_____

If you are overspending consistently, trust yourself enough, love yourself enough to face the facts and agree that there are two ways out of it. You can either make more money or find ways to remove excess costs—maybe a little of both—whatever feels right for you.

Now, let's look at your income. Do you feel good about how much money you make? Are you grateful for your income?

Fostering gratitude for your money is so important. When we are thankful for what we have and express that gratitude, we take ourselves out of wanting what we don't have. And when we express proactive gratitude for what we want in the future, we open a direct path to realizing it and can transform our wanting into knowing. Every time money is deposited into your account, take a moment to feel thankful and cultivate more gratitude.

Please list your current monthly income sources and amounts and reflect on each one with thanksgiving.

_____

_____

_____

As you focus on building a secure financial future, it is helpful to have an idea of your average monthly income and expenses. At the end of this chapter you will find a worksheet to help you discover what your average monthly income and expenses are.

There's no need to track every penny, unless you are among the rare few that love to do this, but I do want you to have the awareness and empowerment of knowing your numbers.

I have found in my own experience that this method gives me boundaries and freedom to stay in charge of our monthly cash flow. Knowing what our average monthly income and costs are—from tracking them—gives me the flexibility to make investments or purchases that are over and above our ordinary costs. Tracking our money flowing to things we love—and with excitement—can bring a whole new attitude toward our money.

Once you learn about the Financial Seasons™ process in Chapter 15, you might choose to apply a season devoted to looking closely at your Value-based Cashflow™. This deeper dive into intentionally tracking your money for a short time frame will provide the data you need to make the best decisions toward your long-term desired outcomes.

Anti-budget success stories

Jesse began investing $300 a month when he realized he didn't want to work forever. Once he looked at his income and fine-tuned how he wanted to spend his money each month to cover his expenses, he felt $300 was

WELCOME TO THE ANTI-BUDGET!

the right amount. Fast-forward 15 years and Jesse has accumulated over $100,000 in his investment account. Jesse feels like he is well on his way to creating his nest egg for the future.

Another client, Stephanie, really wanted to surprise her five kids and take them on a trip to Disney World. She didn't like the idea of paying for it all on a credit card so she decided it was important for her to plan ahead. She priced it out and knew she needed $5,500 for the trip. She broke that down monthly and for the next year saved $458 a month. They had a blast and the best part is, Stephanie doesn't have to dread how she is going to pay off the credit card from the trip.

Angela started her own photography business five years ago. She is thrilled that her income is now higher than she'd ever dreamed. She also feels she has plateaued in the past six months and needs to do something new to increase her revenue.

A friend suggested that Angela invest in herself and join a coaching program designed for entrepreneurs. Angela did her research and discovered the coaching costs $15,000 for a year. She has never invested in something like this and although she feels strongly that it could be the catalyst to helping her go to the next level, the cost scares her.

After looking at her income and expenses and following her intuition for what is right for her, Angela has decided to invest in herself and commit to the program. She knows she is her greatest asset and a good investment. Fast-forward one year and she has doubled her revenue and is enjoying more time freedom based on what she has learned.

I could go on with numerous stories—including my own proof that ***Value-based Cashflow*™** works! This is the anti-budget, as it helps you focus on how you *want* to spend money, and helps you gain the freedom to spend money and track what's important to you. It also encourages you to look at your money in a new way.

Tracking your money should excite you and create a positive experience. It should not feel rigid and annoying. What I have learned is that there will be different seasons in your life in which you will want to pay attention more closely to how you spend money.

MONEY LOVES YOU TOOL

Value-Based Cashflow™ Method

Monthly Income Flow

Primary Income $ _____
Primary Income $ _____
Other Income $ _____
Other Income $ _____
Total Income $ _____

Joy Expenses

_____
_____
_____
_____
_____

Subtotal Expenses $ _____

Annoyance Expenses

_____
_____
_____
_____
_____

Subtotal Expenses $ _____

Name(s) _____

Month _____

Total Expenses
$ _____

Comfort Expenses

_____
_____
_____
_____
_____

Subtotal Expenses $ _____

Download Free Value-Based Cashflow™ PDF

WELCOME TO THE ANTI-BUDGET!

Money Loves You Mindset Principle

Freedom is found in the discipline of boundaries and ensuring you are spending your money on things that genuinely matter to you.

Money loves you because you love the way you are spending your money and investing in yourself now and for the future.

MONEY LOVES YOU NOTE

CHAPTER FIFTEEN

FINANCIAL SEASONS™

Seasons. In nature we have winter, spring, summer, and fall. Our minds understand seasons when it comes to weather. But, often we don't approach life with this seasonal mindset. It is normal that we look at big goals as just that: BIG. We may start toward a big goal and fall short because it is too big, or we feel overwhelmed and it's easier to fall back into our old patterns.

This is tragic with all goals but especially with your money goals. What has been your experience with setting money goals? Have you gotten overwhelmed or frustrated? Have you not felt smart enough? Have you given up because it has been just too hard to gain momentum, or maybe those goals haven't been your priorities?

I have discovered the reasons these money goals are hard to achieve are that the people setting the goals are trying to make too big of a jump, the goal is too black and white, or the goal is too extreme. This puts people in a feast-or-famine, fail-or-succeed, win-or-lose mindset, which makes the goals unachievable in the long run.

The solution to these problems with achieving money goals is not simply to obtain more money. This is a dangerous mindset because it can lead to a never-enough limiting belief. Instead, *managing* money in the way that resonates with you, the way you love to do it, works for achieving your money goals.

You might feel scared to try again with your money goals, or maybe you have lost faith in your ability to understand and work with money. That's okay. Throughout my career, I have walked hundreds of people through their money fears. And I am right here to guide you on your own personalized path. So grab my hand and let's begin because this Financial Seasons™ process will break down setting your money goals into an easy formula for you to follow.

I have found it helpful to think about accomplishing goals as though they were seasons—financial seasons—and you can even name them: this is my saving-for-my-dream-vacation-in-Bahamas season; this is my paying-off-car-loan-so-I-am-free season; this is my establishing-my-emergency-fund-so-I-can-breathe season; this is my investing-in-myself-and-leveling-up season, and so on.

When we can chunk our bigger financial goals—creating financial independence, getting out of debt, saving for the future—into smaller, focused, 90-day seasons, they become more doable.

This exact process has been transformative for my husband and me and we have been using it for the past 18 years. We have seen our net worth go from low six figures to over eight figures. This works and I will teach you how it does.

Each quarter, we look at our Financial Empowerment Snapshot™, review our progress for the past quarter, celebrate what we have accomplished, and if we didn't meet our stated season goals, we examine what went wrong and take the learning from it. No judgment, no regrets or resentment, no excuses, no accusations—we are just curious about what went wrong and we ask ourselves how we can learn from it and then move forward. Not meeting your season goals will happen. Expect it!

Next, we evaluate what is happening in our life and decide mutually what the next season for our money is and what we want to focus on for the next 90 days.

FINANCIAL SEASONS™

Examples of this could be:

- save three months of expenses in a savings account;
- invest $7,000 into a retirement account;
- open a non-retirement investment account and invest $15,000;
- pay off $1,000 of your credit card debt;
- pay off $3,000 of your student loans;
- purchase rental real estate using $100,000 from your savings account;
- save for a dream vacation;
- save for a wedding or other upcoming big expense; or
- save for your children's college education.

The choices are endless. A good place to start is to review your Financial Empowerment Snapshot™ and decide what progress is a priority for you and your family. Pay off debt, increase your assets, or pay for a big upcoming expense are all good examples. If you think about your future financial-self reflection (completed at the end of Chapter 12), what is a good priority that will take you one step closer to your future self?

Once we are mutually aligned with our commitment for the next 90-day season and have named that season, the focused action is the commitment. This action gets integrated into our monthly Value-based Cashflow™ plan, which ensures we maintain our focus on a monthly basis so we can see the progress throughout the season.

Once we commit to the season and what we want our focus to be, the key is to not allow distractions or other goals to pull us off course. You can do and have all the things—you just can't have them all at once. Adding new goals or not honoring your commitment during a season will take you through rough waters and create chaos in your finances. When everything is important, nothing is important. You must keep your commitment as a **single purpose** during your season, knowing that at the end of this season, a new season will begin.

Now we are going to build your Financial Seasons™. What are your most important financial goals for the next 12 months? On the worksheet below name your top 3 to 5 financial aspirations for the next year.

After you have created your annual financial aspirations, sit with them and decide which one(s) makes the most sense to focus on first. There is no right or wrong answer. Which goal(s) do you feel is most important to make progress on? Do you feel good about it? If you don't feel good about it, you won't stick to it. No one can tell you what your priority should be. This is *personal* finance—it's meant to be personal. There is no one-size-fits-all. Once you do this for a few seasons you'll gain momentum and it will become easier and actually enjoyable.

Next, identify your next quarterly season goal(s). It is important that your stated goal for the next 90-day season is crystal clear. For example, you wouldn't say, "I want to pay off debt." You would write, "in the next 90 days, I will pay off $10,000 of my car loan." Be specific; at the end of the season, you'll want to easily be able to know if it's done or not.

Once you are crystal clear on your 90-day goal, break it down even further on the worksheet provided and come up with a strategy of what needs to happen during the 90-days to turn your goal into reality.

FINANCIAL SEASONS™

MONEY LOVES YOU TOOL

Step One: List 3-5 financial aspirations for the next year.

_____

_____

_____

Step Two: Pick one aspiration every quarter over the next year to focus on for the next 90 days.

Write out specifics about the goal you want to achieve so you'll be able to easily know whether or not you completed it by the end. Then, determine the start and end dates for your 90-day season.

My Financial Season: _____	My Financial Season: _____
Start Date: _____ End Date: _____	Start Date: _____ End Date: _____
My Financial Season: _____	My Financial Season: _____
Start Date: _____ End Date: _____	Start Date: _____ End Date: _____

Download Free Financial Season™ PDF

MONEY LOVES YOU

At the end of a Financial Season™, it's time to schedule a date with yourself, your partner, or even your financial coach (if you have one), and evaluate the season. Did you achieve your desired result? If not, what progress did you make? Did you get derailed? What went wrong? It's most important to celebrate both the progress along the journey and the final outcome.

Remember, it is normal for things to go wrong; we are humans. When you start this process, it's new and your Financial Seasons™ could feel like a new diet. Inevitably, when you diet, it is easy to fall off the diet. You eat the cookie and ice cream, which can lead to the mindset of *oh, screw it! I already messed up. Why don't I just eat the whole container of ice cream?* This happens in our subconscious mind so part of this process is exposing it, becoming aware, and choosing to start anew in the moment without more self-sabotaging behavior. It just takes that moment of presence to come back to your superconscious self, extend grace, and recommit to your season. This is not a diet; this is one of your first steps to a new freedom with your finances.

Every day is a new day. Every month is a new month. Things are going to come up and you will need to pivot. Maybe your car breaks down, the dryer quits, or your child needs dental work. This is life and we must embrace it rather than getting angry and then allowing anger to be the beginning of a binge cycle. You are in charge. Choose empowerment!

You can do this. You are smart enough and brilliant. You have everything you need to integrate this into your life and pursue your financial aspirations.

An accountability partner can be a good resource to remind you of exactly this. If you are looking for an accountability partner, we provide one as part of the Inspired Wealth™ Program. Scan the QR code below or visit www.liveinspiredwealth.com to learn more or you can invite a friend to do this process with you and they can be your Financial Seasons™ buddy.

Money Loves You Mindset Principle

When we can chunk our bigger financial goals—creating financial independence, getting out of debt, and saving for the future—into smaller, 90-day Financial Seasons™, they become more doable.

You can do and have all the things— you just can't have them all at once.

MONEY LOVES YOU NOTE

CHAPTER SIXTEEN

RELATIONSHIPS AND MONEY

Money affects every relationship, be it with your partner, children, parents, friends, co-workers, boss, the barista, or the bus driver. Whether you are conscious of it or not, money is a part of relationships. While this chapter will help you strengthen your relationships, that is not where we begin. We first begin with you and your relationship with money.

The more you understand how money works in your life, both in strengths and weaknesses, the more easily you can build a better relationship with yourself and with your money, and as a result, with every person in your life.

With everything you have read so far, my hope is that you have a strong foundation of how money has shaped where you are today and what your money identity is.

Let's take the momentum you've created by looking into your financial mirror and dive down even deeper to a new level. This will allow you to uncover your relationship with money.

What if you treated money like a person? Like an actual relationship? Might seem weird, right? Except, you most likely already do this.

You might call it bad names under your breath or worship it like a loved one, hate it when it doesn't show up, become jealous of others who have it, or think you could never have it. We have already discovered that when you name the truth you get better results.

After working through the concepts and prompts in the Wealth Buster exercise in Chapter 7, you now understand your history with money. What has money taught you in your life? And how do you relate to it? How has it shaped you into who you are today? Is it a power assist or something to be avoided?

Here are some examples of how money can show up in your life as a relationship.

Toxic Control

The stay-at-home wife hates money because she is controlled by it. She has to ask for permission to spend money. She feels unsafe and disconnected from money. Her relationship with money is one filled with fear and shame.

Resentment

The entrepreneur works long hours each day, closing sales and building a team. At the end of the month when all of the employees have been paid, he finds himself exhausted and frustrated that money seems to always be spent and not enough is left over. He feels betrayed by the money and harbors some resentment toward it.

Peace and Patience

The investor enjoys watching her money grow. Each day she spends time nurturing it with her focus and attention. Even on the days when her investments go down, she is patient and understands the nature of investing. Money is a close friend to her and she is there through all the highs and lows.

Gratitude

A small family lives modestly and appreciates all that their simple income provides. Each day when they can buy food for their family and gas for their vehicle to take them where they need to go, they are grateful. Each time the mother turns on the water and water comes out, she feels a sense of security and gratitude for the money that paid the water bill. When the

RELATIONSHIPS AND MONEY

father pays their rent, he feels so grateful for the home his family can live in. He remembers a time when they lived in a cramped apartment and is happy they now have more space to spread out and enjoy time together. Money is a blessing and every penny is accounted for with gratitude.

The above examples illustrate that we have a relationship with money, whether we are aware of it or not. When you can communicate effectively and without judgment about money, you break down other walls. Take a minute to look at how you relate to money.

Does money feel like:

- a faithful partner who is always there to support you?
- a parent who helps you get to where you want to go?
- a villain who is always triggering you, making you feel out of control and hurt?
- an annoying pest that keeps bothering you but won't go away?
- a nagging voice that is always telling you what to do?

Below are a few questions and spaces provided for you to write your answer—right here, right now. It is time for you to discover your true relationship with money.

What is your relationship with money like?

_____

_____

Do you feel like money loves you?

_____

_____

Do you ignore your money?

_____

_____

MONEY LOVES YOU

Do you fear money?

_____

_____

Does money feel annoying to you?

_____

_____

Do you feel ashamed or guilty about money?

_____

_____

I want you to think of your favorite person in the world, right now. Who is it? Did a smile just come to your face? Maybe this person could be your spouse or partner, your mother, your best friend, your favorite aunt, your child. What is amazing about your relationship with this person? What is your favorite thing about this person? Do they inspire you? Make you feel warm inside? Do you feel safe with them? Can you rely on them? Think about the last time you saw this person; how did you feel when they showed up? Got that feeling? Great. Feel it all through your body.

What if this feeling was how you felt toward your money? What if you could have a similar relationship with money that you do with your favorite person? Most likely when you see your favorite person there is an energy of emotion exchanged. Perhaps love, joy, excitement, relief, connection, tenderness, playfulness, curiosity, hope, or belonging could be emotions and energy you experience. That experience of emotion is what I want you to experience in your relationship with money.

If your favorite person is your partner, think back to when you first met them. Were you excited (and maybe nervous) to see them? Did you pick out your clothing very carefully when you went to meet them? Were you highly attuned to what they said, what they did, or how they moved? Maybe your favorite person is your child. How excited were you the day they were born? How attentive were you to their needs? Every sound was new, different, and thrilling (and maybe a little overwhelming at 3 a.m.).

RELATIONSHIPS AND MONEY

It took time, energy, and investment to build toward this beautiful connection you have today in this relationship with your favorite person. We are going to put the same effort into your relationship with money and I know it will leave you empowered and confident with all of your money decisions moving forward. I have created a framework that will guide you in building a strong foundation for the money success ahead.

Most of you reading this will have been on some form of a date. A date doesn't have to be romantic. Have you ever taken yourself out to dinner and a movie or on a beautiful walk or hike in nature? How about going with a group of friends for a fun night out? Great dates have planning, intention, fun, excitement, and adventure all baked into the experience.

This section will support you whether you are in a relationship, dating, single, going through a divorce, or experiencing a loss. Your relationship with money is just that: yours. It's personal. This process will support you in whatever stage of life you find yourself. So, let's get to building that great relationship.

Money Loves You Relationship Building Process

If you have completed the exercises in this book, you've already accomplished the first part of the process. Grab your money stories from Chapter 7 and continue to build on this work.

Part I: Get Clear

Money Loves You

- Schedule an intentional time with yourself.
- Journal your money stories. See prompts in Chapter 7 to assist.
- Reflect back on what you wrote. Read without developing comments or opinions.
- Ask clarifying questions of yourself. Quick tip: this could be a place for a Wealth Buster to show up.
- Listen to yourself with kindness. Let yourself be heard.
- Decide what you want your relationship with money to be.

Part II: Set it Up

Money Loves You Date Framework

- Select a day and time (weekly, bimonthly, or monthly) to dedicate to your Money Loves You Date that will be free from the distractions of business, kids, texts, or emails.

- Choose a location that you enjoy. Make this an experience that you will love. If you are single, where do you find the most joy? Are you adventurous? Do you like being outside or would you prefer to be cuddled up with a favorite beverage? If you are dating, could you imagine going on a Money Loves You Date with this person? If you are with a partner, where do the two of you feel the most connected? Is there a special place that brings you both joy and laughter? Is there an outfit that makes you feel great? Wear that! Pick a location that you love. Create the experience that brings you joy, and take yourself (and your partner) out on a date to meet with your money.

- Before you go on this date, be thoughtful and intentional about using loving words toward yourself and your partner (if it is a shared date). Focus on eliminating language that could create feelings of shame or guilt for any actions or inactions that have occurred that month.

- Use the Inspired Wealth™ tools to help you navigate your communication and create success with your money. These tools empower you in the managing and investing of your finances.

Part III: Go Out!

Money Loves You Date Agenda

- Review your Value-based Cashflow™ report.
    - What progress have you made since your last date?
    - What did you love spending money on?
    - Are there any frustrations or struggles to discuss?
    - What went well and can be celebrated?

- Look at your progress with the current Financial Season™ you are in (refer to Chapter 15).
    - Do any changes need to be made to make your Financial Season™ focus a success?
- Once a quarter review and update your Financial Empowerment Snapshot™.

The more time you spend with your money in a loving way, the stronger your relationship will be. Doing this work sets you up to be financially independent. Following these guidelines and the framework outlined above, while using the Inspired Wealth™ tools, creates profound safety in your relationships and ultimately brings you to the level of success you desire.

Advice for readers who are single

I have witnessed many go through divorce or loss of a partner and discover that they no longer feel controlled by their finances. This newfound perceived freedom has resulted in many of my clients rebelling and spending money without awareness. This is completely normal, and I invite you to not shame yourself if this has been the case for you.

Instead, think about how your future self will be hurt and affected by your choices. Ask yourself, *how can I redirect my energy to making empowered decisions with my money.*

Being single and working with money can be great and maintaining momentum can be simple without anyone else impacting it. It could also be lonely, as money isn't something that is normally discussed with friends. Having someone other than yourself to coach, guide, or relate with about your money can be very beneficial.

Advice for readers who are dating

I would imagine money is the last thing you want to talk about when you're dating someone new. Although, traditionally, money isn't a romantic topic, I challenge you to think how it could be. Imagine feeling so confident in your relationship with money (because you've done all the work in these pages) that the result is freedom and empowerment. Freedom to share your financial goals and aspirations enables you to state exactly what your future self wants and what you are doing to get there. This confidence is an attractor. The matter then becomes, *are they a match for you*, and *have they done this work*? Why or why not? Are they willing to have conversations about money?

Money alignment can have a significant impact on the success of your future relationship. So, maybe not on the first date, but I would encourage you to ask about their financial goals sooner than later. Be bold!

It is critical to not ignore your money. Doing this work sets you up to pursue financial independence, whether you find your perfect mate or not. As you grow wealth and become more empowered with money, you will evolve into being a match for your ideal partner.

Advice for readers with children

Make a conscious effort to have a healthy relationship with the topic of money and your kids. If you feel the timing is right, invite your kids on a Money Loves You Date. Let them be involved in picking the location and details. Make it a game for them and *you*!

You could introduce the concept of thinking about your future self to them as they start wanting to purchase items at stores or online. Let your child's imagination be free in asking, "Would my future self agree to this purchase, this investment, or this decision?"

Our children remember our actions far more easily than they remember our words. Getting them involved with how you think and work with money is an incredible gift to them. I am writing this book today because of the foundations my parents showed me in my first 18 years of life.

Advice for readers with a spouse or partner

As with any great relationship, there is an element of fun. Imagine that this is a game that the two of you are playing together. Below are some boundaries (because rules don't work) to help both of you to succeed and build abundance together!

The Game of Relationship Abundance

- Unless you are both totally comfortable talking about money in bed, keep the bedroom a space for emotional connection, relaxation, and intimacy. It should be off limits for money conversations.

RELATIONSHIPS AND MONEY

- Don't talk about money with your partner when you do a quick check of the bank account and see a ton of debits you weren't aware of. Keep these for your dates.
- Don't have drive-by money conversations. For example, your partner is cooking dinner and you say, "Hey babe, I know we have been looking at getting a new car to replace the one that keeps breaking down. I am thinking of going to the dealership tomorrow and buying a new car. What do you think?" Again, leave this for your date. If something is urgent, schedule an emergency Money Loves You Date.
- If talking about money is new to you, only discuss money during your financial date.

Helpful tip: make notes for your date if something comes up in between dates.

Many people struggle with the topic of money in their relationships. If you have ever gone to a marriage counselor, you know the most common advice given is: if you want to heal your relationship, you first must work on yourself.

If you are in a relationship where your partner manages the money and you find yourself thinking you don't need to pay attention, or you are ignoring the money altogether, choose to change this! It is your responsibility to really own your actions with your money and become a master with your finances. I have had a number of clients find themselves suddenly single, by death or divorce, and only wishing they knew how to handle their finances. Furthermore, they don't have the slightest idea of what their financial picture even looks like.

Let me now finish the rest of the story I told in the beginning of this book about how I used to hide my shopping bags from my hubby. I want to share how far we've come.

Today, when I make a new purchase or when all the boxes show up on our porch, I don't hide them at all. I shout with joy, "Babe, look what I got!" He gives me that little smile and says, "Show me." It's like Christmas as I open the package and try on or display the contents. It becomes a special moment between us without feelings of guilt or shame.

So what has changed in 25 years? We cleared out our own Wealth Busters and created a relationship with money that led to a deep trust in ourselves, trust in each other, and trust in this process. We did the individual work to invest in our future selves, aligned our visions, and as partners, together we have built financial independence.

This didn't happen overnight for us and that is a good thing! Most lottery winners lose their fortunes within a few years. We started this process in 2005 and even made zero, if not negative, progress in some of our Financial Seasons™. You don't have to be perfect but you do have to keep going.

Aligning your financial vision with your partner's makes your relationship that much more powerful. Your relationship to money will be the activator to the success you desire.

Chris became an active participant in our money conversations and I overcame my own lack of self-worth and guilt. We were willing to have the hard conversations, listen generously to one another, and overcome the limiting beliefs that held us back early on in our relationship.

We now decide together what our financial aspirations are and how we will accomplish them in each season. Watching our Financial Empowerment Snapshot™ grow over the years has been exciting to experience with my husband. This growth and change has inspired both of us to play, create memories, and have fun in the present and also build a strong financial foundation for our future that allows us to give generously and ensure our legacy is sound.

When you can communicate about money effectively and without judgment, you break down walls and ultimately provide the ability and confidence to speak straight about other taboo subjects. When two people are aligned using these principles, they can create exponential growth in their abundance and relationship.

This chapter might be the most important of all. If you take it to heart and implement the process, you will see all of your relationships thrive.

Money Loves You Mindset Principle

Whether you are conscious of it or not,
money is a part of relationships.

The more you understand how money works in your life, both in strengths and weaknesses, the more easily you can build a better relationship with yourself and with your money, and as a result, with every person in your life.

MONEY LOVES YOU NOTE

CHAPTER SEVENTEEN

HERE IS WHAT IS NOW POSSIBLE

I am celebrating you and all that you have accomplished so far! You have cleared out your Wealth Busters, looked into your financial mirror to see the truth, cleaned out that cluttered financial closet, and found your numbers through the Inspired Wealth™ process. You've created your first Financial Season™, which has helped you gain a clear focus and set secure boundaries.

So now we get to talk about ALL that is possible for you from here on out. When you have a solid financial base, you are able to really create abundant wealth through multiple facets and streams of income.

Over my career in helping hundreds of clients who are doctors, nurses, teachers, linemen, plumbers, and business owners, I have seen a common theme: their goal of becoming millionaires. This is such a rewarding and fun journey to witness as my team and I have advised and coached our clients in pursuing their financial goals, quarter after quarter, until they become their future millionaire self.

Some grow their assets to their future millionaire self and then it's as if the switch is turned off. They made it! So, they start to coast.

Others use their money to generate more money instead of living off their income from their investments. They generate multiple streams of income. Maybe it's rental real estate properties, a business that generates cash flow, or investments in income-focused strategies. There are numerous ways available to you.

Personal finance is personal and just one way is not right or wrong; you get to decide. At each point along your financial journey, as your assets and net worth grow, different opportunities arise. *Money meets you where you are and matches your desires.*

As you've experienced while reading this book, changing your thoughts, beliefs, and actions around building financial freedom is like a full-body makeover for your mind and your money. You can do it on your own, but support makes it so much easier.

Find support.

In Chapter 6, you saw how the best people in any given field use coaches to reach their goals. Hiring a coach gives you an incentive to ensure this book was not just a motivational read or a short-lived phase. My hope is that this book leaves you with long-lasting inspiration, that you'll continually implement the strategies and tools, and that you've found a new way to move forward with your money.

In my financial advisory firm, Financial Freedom Wealth Management Group, we have helped people at all levels of wealth understand their Financial Empowerment Snapshot™, identify their aspirations, create tailored strategies, and guide them into their future financial selves.

Financial Freedom Wealth Management Group's Inspired Wealth™ program is designed to help you implement all the tools from this book as well as give you specialized advice in areas that are more complex (or that I didn't address in this book), such as investment management, family wealth and estate planning, tax reduction planning, business exit planning, and retirement income and distribution planning.

Seeking help from a qualified professional, such as a licensed financial advisor, brings a powerful new perspective to your financial life. It also provides you with new avenues and tools to help you manage your money. We have found that when our clients partner with us, they feel a supportive collaboration in their wealth journey. We provide ease in helping them with

HERE IS WHAT IS NOW POSSIBLE...

their investment choices as well as financial guidance. This also creates accountability in working toward their financial goals.

If you want a licensed financial coach and advisor who will walk beside you, empower you with your money decisions, and help you live the principles in this book, then I invite you to check out my amazing team at Financial Freedom Wealth Management Group and our Inspired Wealth™ program. Scan the QR Code to learn more.

Not only will you be getting the support you need but you will be joining a community of like-minded individuals who want to build abundance through the principles in this book.

Whether you hire my team as your financial coach and advisor or already work with one currently, I encourage you to find someone that uses the principles discussed here. Ensure they take time to listen to and hear you as you share about your current financial life and how it has an impact on you and your future. Ensure they don't use fear, shame, or scare tactics to try to motivate you.

Love is always the answer with our money.

When you have a safe relationship with your financial advisor and coach, you should be able to share openly and vulnerably about what is going on in your financial life. They need to listen generously and guide you along the journey.

My wish for you is that you get the support you need. Money loves you when you love you. Embracing this will bring feelings of joy, happiness, and freedom.

I want you to know that there is so much more ahead for you now. By reading this book and putting what I have taught you into action, your future has immediately shifted. Your present-day situation will soon look and feel different. **Wealth begins with how you feel and then**

translates into new actions that ultimately create a whole new life.

This moment, **right here**, is a moment I want you to remember: the moment when your life shifted into you being the driver of your financial freedom. This is the beginning of a whole new way of being.

HERE IS WHAT IS NOW POSSIBLE . . .

Money Loves You Mindset Principle

Personal finance is personal and just one way
is not right or wrong; you get to decide.

*Wealth begins with how you feel,
and then translates into new actions
that ultimately create a whole new life.*

MONEY LOVES YOU NOTE

CHAPTER EIGHTEEN

ALLOW MONEY TO LOVE YOU

This book can be just that—a book. OR . . . you could let it be the transformation that changes your life forever.

It is time to start creating your future. The hardest part of change is getting started and once you gain momentum, the change is easier to maintain. If you have read this far, you have most likely experienced change and momentum and have redefined your relationship with money.

I know that you have had your own personal past experience with money that was unique to you. As you have journeyed through these pages, you have seen, named, and released your old relationship to money, allowing for more room in your heart to receive.

To receive more.

More abundance, more love, more memories, more trust in yourself and your financial decisions, more streams of income, more security, and more hope for a wonderful future ahead.

You have done the work to open up space for you to *receive*.

There is one final principle I will leave you with as we come to the end of our time together in this book.

It is the most simple yet most important of all.

If you want to receive more, **you must ask**.

Ask and you will receive.

"Ask, and it shall be given you; seek, and ye shall find; knock, and it shall be opened unto you" (Luke 11:9, King James Version).

This promise is one that many great thought leaders have shared over the years. And it is one that I myself will stamp as a true principle of abundance.

Ask for what you want.

Desire and **seek** how to find it.

And then **take action** and it will be given to you.

These three simple sentences encompass all that is within these pages.

I invite you to write these words and place them where you can read them often. Remember that you now have everything you need to create the present-day and future-day realities of your dreams.

As you are fully empowered with the tools and principles you need to build lifelong wealth, I want to complete this book with one final action.

I want you to be able to see all the progress you have achieved as you have read through these pages and walked this path with me. I find it is easy to forget to see our own personal growth. We often are looking ahead and forget to see how far we have actually come. But what I have noticed is that if you can witness your progress, you will be able to move toward your future with more momentum, hope, and faith.

This final action step has three parts.

- **Part 1**. Write where you were mentally, emotionally, relationally, and financially when you began reading this book.

- **Part 2**. Write out where you are right now in all the same spaces—mentally, emotionally, relationally, and financially—since you have completed reading this book.
- **Part 3**. Where will you be in the future?

Let's begin this process.

Part 1: Where I Was

When I began reading this book, this is where I was: Revisit Chapter 7 and your original Wealth Buster statements you circled.

Mentally

_____

_____

Emotionally

_____

_____

Relationally

_____

_____

Financially

_____

_____

Other than above, other thoughts or feelings I experienced about where I was when I began this book are:

_____

_____

_____

_____

Part 2: Current State

Now that I have completed reading Money Loves You, here is where I am now:

Mentally

_____

_____

Emotionally

_____

_____

Relationally

_____

_____

Financially

_____

_____

Any other thoughts regarding how I currently feel?

_____

_____

_____

Part 3: My Future

Here is what I see possible for my future now that I have read *Money Loves You*.

Mentally

_____

_____

Emotionally

_____

_____

Relationally

_____

_____

Financially

_____

_____

What dreams and aspirations do I now have for my future? Write out the future you are now living into.

_____

_____

_____

How does this feel?

_____

_____

_____

I see so many possibilities in our world when we embrace more love. Money is an essential part of our daily lives. We can't ignore it, we can't turn away from it, and we can't delegate it to someone else; we have to be the one who takes authority over it.

When we have love, fear cannot exist. When we know money loves us, it doesn't have power over us. It doesn't become an obsession. It doesn't make us greedy or manipulative. It's simply peace.

When we take on this responsibility and begin to heal our relationships with money, we heal our relationships with ourselves, our partners, our parents, our children, our friends.

Imagine with me the ripple effect of this.

Remember: Money loves you.

PS: I would love to hear from you and how this book has impacted your life. Please feel free to tag me on social media and use the hashtag #MoneyLovesYou

MY FINAL LOVE NOTE OF ACKNOWLEDGEMENT

With my deepest gratitude and acknowledgement, I want to thank my hubby, Chris. You have been my biggest supporter and I'm so appreciative of your willingness to allow me to share our stories to help others. Your unwavering belief in me has fueled my passion and given me the strength to get through the ups and downs. Cheers to many more years of shared dreams, laughter, and adventures. I love you.

To my parents, Jim and Jane Szabo, thank you for instilling in me a strong foundation of faith and for raising me to love God. Your guidance extended beyond spiritual matters, as you also taught me essential financial principles. These teachings have not only shaped my understanding of money but have paved the way for my purpose and career—helping others manage their finances. I am deeply grateful for the values and knowledge you've imparted, which continue to influence and guide me on this journey. I love you both.

To my children: Katelyn, Jasmine, and Jake. You inspire me to be the best version of myself everyday. Your boundless energy, curiosity, and unwavering love fill my life with so much joy and purpose. As I watch each of you grow and navigate the world in your unique ways, I am reminded of the incredible privilege it is to be your mom. I love you kiddos.

To Keira Brinton, I will never forget our author's adventure and the magical way you helped me bring this book to life. I am awed by your faith and love for bringing people's stories to the world. Your dedication, passion, and unwavering belief in this project have made the journey unforgettable. Working together has been an inspiring collaboration, and I am deeply grateful for the expertise, guidance, and creativity you brought to every step of the process.

To Natalee Bloom, for your brilliant mind, championing my voice and bringing so much enthusiasm to my book, thank you.

To Lisa Haukom, Ashley Catalfamo, Amy Carlson, Taylor Isaac, and Angel Harris, thank you for being my first readers of this book. Your feedback helped craft my words to ensure the best end result. I appreciate your time, care, friendship, and love.

To Jason Harris, Jennifer Webster, and my team at Financial Freedom Wealth Management Group who have supported my vision for this book and our Inspired Wealth™ platform, thank you for helping us build such an extraordinary company.

And finally, to my clients who have allowed me and my team to care deeply about you and your financial lives, thank you. We are honored by the trust you have in us and are committed to helping you pursue financial freedom and independence.

EXTRA RESOURCES

As I continue to develop tools and resources to enhance your wealth-building journey, I am committed to sharing them with you.

Scan the QR code below to access the tools featured in this book, as well as expanded resources I want to share with you.

CONNECT WITH JULIA

🌐 www.juliamcarlson.com

▶ youtube.com/@juliacarlson_

📷 @julia.carlson_

f facebook.com/juliamcarlson1

in www.linkedin.com/in/juliamcarlson/

BUSINESS WEBSITE:
www.financialfreedomwmg.com and
www.freedomtaxllc.com

INSPIRED WEALTH™ PLATFORM:
www.liveinspiredwealth.com

PODCAST:
link.chtbl.com/financiallyfree

Made in United States
Orlando, FL
23 July 2024